The BATTLE OF LAKE GEORGE

The
BATTLE
OF
LAKE GEORGE

*England's First Triumph in the
French and Indian War*

WILLIAM R. GRIFFITH IV

THE
History
PRESS

Published by The History Press
Charleston, SC
www.historypress.net

Front cover: The Battle of Lake George by Frederick Coffay Yohn, 1905. *Author's collection.*
Back cover: General Johnson Saving a Wounded French Officer from the Tomahawk of a North American Indian. Author's collection.
Insert: Sir William Johnson. Courtesy of Library of Congress.

First published 2016

ISBN 9781540200174

Library of Congress Control Number: 2016936699

I would like to dedicate this book to my loving family; past mentor, Dr. Mark Snell; and to all those who were there along the way but are no longer by my side. Thank you.

CONTENTS

ACKNOWLEDGEMENTS

$\mathcal{P}$iecing together the story of the Battle of Lake George was something that was not completed overnight. Such a complicated subject in a very misunderstood period of our nation's history required years of reading and research in order for me to gain a comfortable grasp of what had transpired in the summer of 1755. Writing from West Virginia, it was even more difficult to explain something that happened hundreds of miles away. Thanks to the Internet and years of collecting primary and secondary sources, the task was made somewhat easier.

Along the way I received a tremendous amount of support from my peers and professors at Shepherd University. They inspired me to expand on a smaller paper that I had written on the battle for a military history class in 2012. With a push from one of my past professors, Dr. Matthew Foulds, I presented my analysis at the Phi Alpha Theta Mid-Atlantic Regional Conference at George Washington University in April 2014. My argument was well received, and I was determined to expand my work into a book-length study.

Much of my research was done during my time spent as an intern and volunteer at the David Library of the American Revolution in Washington Crossing, Pennsylvania, which includes an incredible amount of primary and secondary sources relating to the colonial era that can leave one in awe. The library's staff members are some of the most helpful and knowledgeable people that you can meet, and I would like to give a special thanks to Meg McSweeney for giving me the opportunity to work there and to librarian

Kathie Ludwig for introducing me to the various collections and for supporting my endeavor as well.

I would also like to thank my amazing past coworkers at Fort Frederick State Park in Big Pool, Maryland. During the summer of 2015, I was fortunate enough to be given the opportunity to interpret the French and Indian War to the general public and also had my eyes opened to a different side of the conflict that I had not previously studied: material culture. Before my time at Fort Frederick I was strictly a military historian who only focused on battlefield strategy, tactics and so on. But now I have been introduced to a type of history that really brings things down to a personal level with the common soldier. It was an incredible experience to be able to interpret a flintlock musket and the various duties performed by men garrisoning the fort.

Without the proper education and guidance it is impossible for one to exert himself to his full potential. Since my first day at Shepherd University, Dr. Mark Snell served not only as an advisor and professor to me but also as a mentor. He taught me to be disciplined as an historian and to observe things objectively. He forced me to open myself up to all aspects of military history and to never be afraid to accept criticism from my academic peers or be deterred from my beliefs when others do not necessarily agree with my arguments. He shaped me into the historian that I am today and will be for the rest of my life. For that I am ever grateful.

While much of the research was done on my own, I did not keep my interpretations and findings to myself. My friends and family were always eager to hear how my work was progressing and were always there to listen to my thoughts regarding my own work. This past year has not been easy, and I owe it to my family and friends for helping me overcome all adversity and for pushing me to never give up or lose sight of my dreams.

I would also like to personally thank my fraternity brothers of Lambda Chi Alpha for being my family away from my family and always supporting me and showing interest in what I love. Along with them, I am forever in debt toward my history colleagues and friends Kevin Pawlak and Mike Galloway for assisting me with all types of research for various topics, for always being open to a good discussion and for walking the battlefields of our great country with me at every given opportunity.

Finally, I would like to give a very special thanks to my family for making me the man I am today. Without their love and support none of this would be possible.

INTRODUCTION

*T*he significance of a historical event can never be fully understood if it is isolated from its greater context. On a hot summer day in September 1755 at the southern end of Lake George, located amid the beautiful northern woodlands of Upstate New York's Adirondack Mountains, an army of colonists then fighting beside the British Empire scored a victory for King George II, the consequences and importance of which have since been misunderstood or neglected by historians and students of military history alike. In the centuries following the Battle of Lake George, scholars have failed to place the event in the greater context of the French and Indian War and more precisely the "undeclared" war being waged in 1755 between England and France for control of the North American continent. The engagement is constantly interpreted as an isolated event as remote as the virgin northern forests and is described as an insignificant victory that was part of a larger military campaign failure. However, this victory achieved much more than just securing the southern end of Lake George for the English—ground on which the construction of Fort William Henry would begin immediately following the battle. The victory itself is extremely unique, and the consequences of what could have happened had the French driven Sir William Johnson's army from the field may very well have spelled disaster for British expansion efforts on the continent.

In 1903, historian Morris Patterson Ferris concluded in his *Account of the Battle of Lake George, September 8, 1755*, that the fighting that day "was the first great successful battle fought wholly by the provincial troops, and the most important fought on New York soil prior to the Revolution." He could not have been more right when describing the victory in this manner. It truly was one of the first "American" battlefield victories in North America. Only one British regular officer served among the ranks of Johnson's army, which was made up entirely of volunteers and militia conscripts from New England and New York. These "farmer soldiers," as Ferris described them, stood muzzle to muzzle against a French army consisting of regular grenadiers as well as Canadian militia and Native Americans who were accustomed to fighting in the North American wilderness. By the end of the day they had emerged victorious, driving the enemy from the field and capturing the general officer in command of all His Most Christian Majesty's regular troops in the colonies, Jean Armand, Baron de Dieskau.[1]

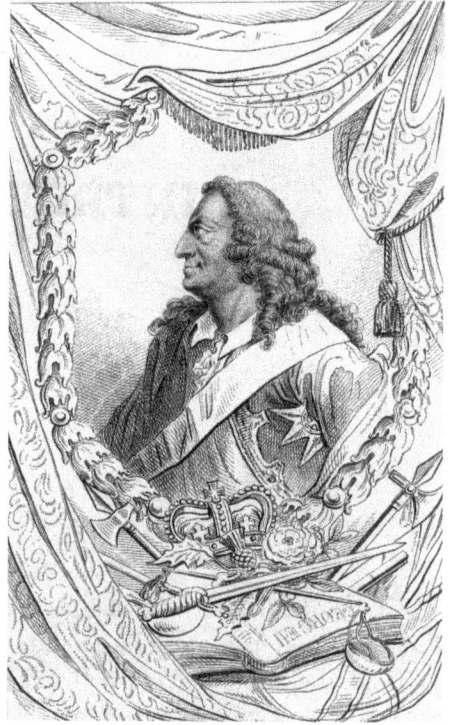

His Majesty King George II of England. *Courtesy of New York Public Library Digital Collections.*

Many historians writing in the past fifty years or so have gone as far as describing the engagement at Lake George as a stalemate and insignificant because the overall campaign against French Fort St. Frédéric at Crown Point astride Lake Champlain failed. The battle was not a stalemate at all in a tactical sense or even a strategic sense. Any time an army drives its adversary from the field and gains full possession of it, victory can be declared—this is the definition of a tactical victory. Strategically, although the battle did not capture the stone fort at Crown Point, it did prevent the French from proceeding any farther south into the interior of the colony of New York and sent them scurrying back north, where they then began erecting another fort on the rise of ground between Lakes George and Champlain known as Ticonderoga, thus ending their campaign against the British for the year. With no major overland road networks leading north into Canada during the French and Indian War, waterways would have to serve as military highways in which large armies with their supply trains could advance up or down between New France and the English colonies. Lake George, thirty-two miles long, was one of those waterways leading north into Canada from New York City, which would eventually become one of three permanent supply bases in the colonies used to equip and provision the British armies in the field. The Battle of Lake George secured this avenue of advance for use in campaigns that would take place in the upcoming years of conflict. Writing six years after Ferris about the battle around its sesquicentennial, when interest in the event seemed to find a new birth, Henry Taylor Blake argued that Lake George was "one of the most desperate battles and important victories in our colonial history." If what Blake claims is in fact true, why is so little known of the fighting that took place in Upstate New York on September 8, 1755?[2]

My journey studying the French and Indian War, and more particularly the New York theater of war, began in the summer of 1997 when I was all but five years old. Although my understanding of where I was and what I was actually viewing was most likely nonexistent at the time, I always date my introduction to history to this first visit to Fort William Henry. Growing older while vacationing at Lake George every year, I began to develop a fascination with the colonial history of the region and romanticize about the once-vast wilderness that was North America and with our forefathers who inhabited it. While visiting the site of the 1757 siege and ensuing "massacre" each year, I was oblivious to the fact that located directly beside the reconstructed Vauban-style timber fort was a battlefield. Although the whole area that comprises the present-day Lake George Village is technically a "battlefield" (the French trenches from the weeklong siege literally were dug under what today are souvenir shops, roads and sidewalks), the Lake George Battlefield Park comprises the site of the 1755 engagement between Dieskau and Johnson. For someone who is not familiar with the regional history of Lake George or the French and Indian War, it is very easy to overlook the significance of the site.

The publication of James Fenimore Cooper's *The Last of the Mohicans* in 1826 and subsequent releases of cinematic adaptations in the twentieth century introduced the general public to the story of Fort William Henry. The powerful influence of film and literature on historical memory has left the Battle of Lake George standing in the shadow of the "massacre" and 1757 siege. Today, visitors who walk the fort's parade ground are indulged in garrison life of an army during the French and Indian War—the men, uniforms, arms and accoutrements. But few are introduced to the reasons that

William Henry stood where it did. All of these questions can be answered by simply walking to the Lake George Battlefield Park, where a wide-open field, beautiful monuments and interpretive waysides tell the story of the bitter struggle that transpired between two empires in 1755. While the park—the site of the second engagement of the battle—seems to be in plain sight, the ground where the first and final actions of September 8, 1755, located astride modern-day Route 9, is even more widely missed and overlooked.

This book is not meant to be a groundbreaking study on the subject, but is more an accessible introduction to the battle and the first full year of fighting during the French and Indian War in North America. Using primary sources and the work of scholars throughout the past century and a half or so, this work will piece together the story of the battle and place it within the bigger picture of events transpiring during the middle of the eighteenth century. This will also serve to enhance the knowledge and understanding of the region's role and importance within the colonial history of America. For centuries Upstate New York has given birth to stories of heroism and sacrifice, tragedy and triumph. These tales of empire and freedom are part of the fabric of the American nation—everything that makes the country's journey to the present day so unique. The Battle of Lake George is no exception to this. It truly is a remarkable story torn from the pages of history that deserves to be recognized as a defining moment of colonial America.

1

THE CARLYLE HOUSE CONGRESS, APRIL 1755

*I*t had been nearly a year since hostilities between England and France erupted along the Ohio River Valley at Jumonville Glen and Fort Necessity, and now events began to unfold that would eventually hurl the two great nations against each other in a war that would decide the fate of North America and the greater part of the world. Although open warfare had not officially been declared, steps were being taken by both sides to ensure that their colonial possessions would be secure and held firmly in their hands against any encroaching adversaries. In Alexandria, Virginia, Major General Edward Braddock, newly appointed commander in chief of His Majesty's Forces in North America, arrived from Williamsburg poised to meet with the colonial governors to present the plans for the coming summer campaign against French military strongholds in the Great Lakes region, Ohio River Valley, Nova Scotia and along the Lake Champlain corridor. The expeditions, if properly executed, were meant to be a four-pronged offensive that would completely oust the French from land that King George II believed rightfully belonged to England.

On April 14–15, 1755, that plan was laid out to those personalities present in the parlor of Ohio Company member John Carlyle's impressive Virginia home.[3] In attendance at this congress were the royal governors of five colonies that were set to take part in the coming expeditions: Horatio Sharpe of Maryland, William Shirley of Massachusetts, James DeLancey of New York, Robert Morris of Pennsylvania and Robert Dinwiddie of Virginia. Maryland, Pennsylvania and Virginia were to supply troops and provisions for Braddock's own expedition against Fort Duquesne at the Forks of the Ohio River, while Massachusetts and New York would give their assistance to the efforts against the northern objectives. While Braddock and a twenty-four-hundred-man force of British Regular and colonial provincial troops moved west from Alexandria and Frederick, Maryland, to expel the French from the Ohio River Valley, three other major French strongholds were to be targeted by a trio of British colonial armies.[4]

Guarding Chignecto Isthmus—the narrow strip of land connecting Nova Scotia to the mainland of Canada— was a large pentagonal fort built in the early 1750s in response to British

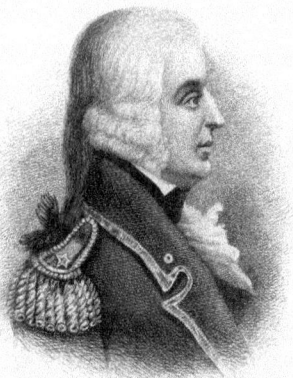

Major General Edward Braddock.
Courtesy of Library of Congress.

desires to Anglicize Nova Scotia by promoting Protestant immigration to the region. The capitulation of Fort Beauséjour was a critical objective for the submission of French influence in Nova Scotia and more specifically in Acadia in 1755. "Gov[ernor] Shirley," according to Braddock in a letter written several days following the Alexandria meeting, "lay'd before me the Measures concerted between him and Gov[ernor] Charles Lawrence [of Nova Scotia] for repelling the French from their new Encroachments on the Bay of Fund[y], which I approv'd of, and immediately sent orders to Lt. Colonel [Robert] Monckton to take upon him that Command and carry it into execution."[5] The expedition would be made up of a majority of New England provincial troops, and their jumping-off point would be British-held Fort Lawrence, located roughly a half day's march from the French at Fort Beauséjour. While Monckton and his men advanced into Nova Scotia and Braddock's expedition cut its way through the Virginia and Pennsylvania wilderness, two more armies were set to assail the French along Lakes Champlain and Ontario.

William Shirley had previously helped raise and command various expeditions during English and French colonial wars the decade prior. His experience did not necessarily make him an ideal candidate for a high-ranking position in 1755, but Braddock nonetheless appointed him second-in-command and gave him the task of mustering a colonial force strong

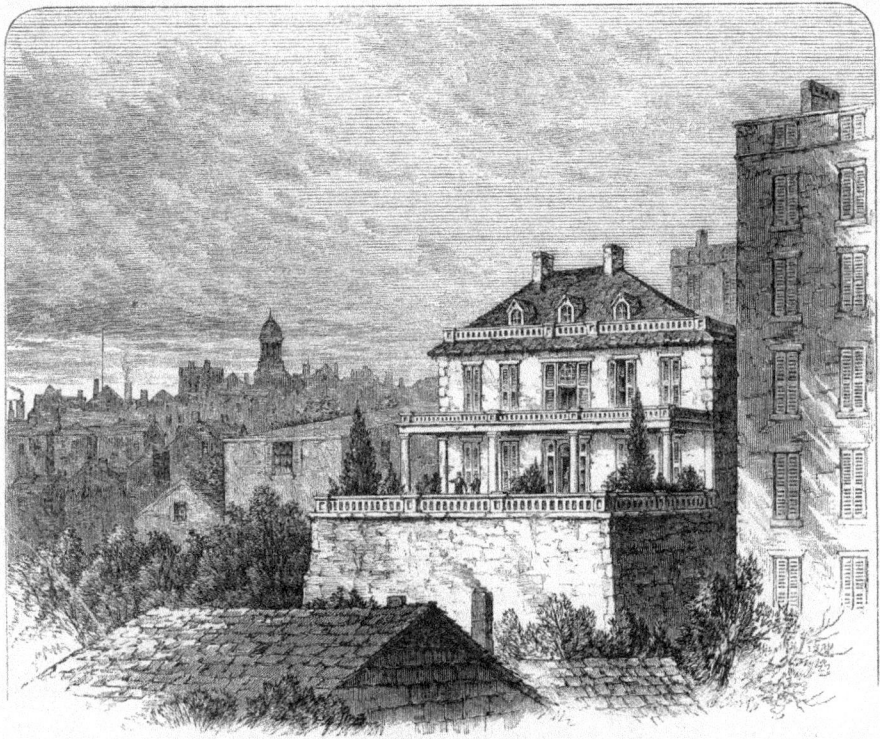

THE BRADDOCK HOUSE, ALEXANDRIA, VA.

The John Carlyle House. *Courtesy of New York Public Library Digital Collections.*

enough to move west to Lake Ontario and capture the French stronghold of Fort Niagara. "[Shirley] express'd the greatest Readiness to engage in it," Braddock recorded after the meetings. "I therefore order'd him to take his own Regiment [Fiftieth Regiment of Foot] which is compleat, and Sir William Pepperell's [Fifty-first Regiment of Foot] which will probably be so too by the time he wants them, and to proceed upon it as soon as possible with my orders to reinforce the Garrison at Oswego [located along the southeastern shore of Lake Ontario] . . . and put the Works in such Repair as to preserve the Garrison and secure his Retreat and Convoys."[6] Shirley's army of colonial troops placed on the British military establishment—which made them Regular Regiments—and a battalion of New Jersey Blues (First New Jersey Regiment) were ordered to organize at the major supply base of Albany, New York, before moving west to Fort Oswego. There, too, would be another army of New Englanders and New Yorkers poised to move north toward Lake Champlain and the French-held Fort St. Frédéric, known to the British as Crown Point. They, like so many colonial provincial soldiers, were an army of amateurs destined to take on one of the mightiest military forces in the modern world and some of the best wilderness warriors the North American continent had ever seen. The reduction of these two French strongholds was crucial to British military success in 1755.

London's official instructions for the capitulations of Forts Niagara and Crown Point, given to Edward Braddock in November 1754 before he departed for North America, were as follows:

> *If you should find, that the two British Regiments* [Forty-fourth and Forty-eighth Regiments of Foot] *will be sufficient for performing the service at Niagara* [after reducing Fort Duquesne], *you may, then, employ the two American Regiments* [Fiftieth and Fifty-first Regiments of Foot], *at the same time, in dispossessing the French from their Post at Crown Point, on Lake* [Champlain], *which is the next point you will endeavor to gain; But no positive instructions can be given you, upon this head, as you can only judge, hereafter, whether such a separate operation can be undertaken, at the same time, that you are making yourself Master of that most material one, at Niagara. However after you shall have possessed yourself of the Niagara Forts, and shall have opened a safe communication betwixt that, and Oswego (which will not only secure the Back settlements, but likewise, bring back those Indians, who have fallen off from Our interest, and joined the French;) It is our will and pleasure, that the next service upon which you shall proceed, shall be . . . The reducing of the Fort at Crown Point, and erecting another upon the Lake* [Champlain], *in such place as you shall find most effectual for bridling the French Indians in those parts and for securing and protecting, our neighboring Colonies.*[7]

Braddock's orders were much simpler on paper than they would be to execute. After moving his army over three hundred miles from Virginia, he was to steamroll his way over the French at Fort Duquesne, move north and capture Fort Niagara, then move east and assist the provincial expedition set to capture Crown Point, all the while obtaining the support of the Indians, whose French "Father" had been expelled from those regions. If all went well, the provincial armies in New York would need not undertake their expeditions alone without the support of the superiorly trained British Regulars and the watchful eye of General Braddock.[8]

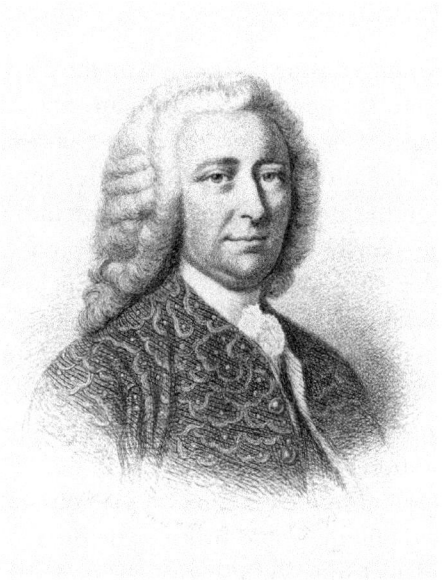

Left: William Shirley, royal governor of Massachusetts and Braddock's second-in-command. *Courtesy of New York Public Library Digital Collections.*

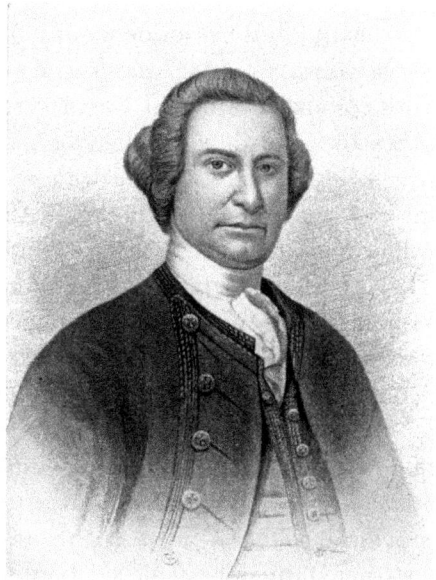

Right: Sir William Johnson, superintendent of Indian affairs in the Northern Colonies and commanding general of the Crown Point expeditionary force. *Courtesy of Library of Congress.*

Present in Alexandria those two April days in 1755 alongside the royal governors, William Johnson, a forty-year-old New Yorker of Irish descent and one of the most respected advocates of colonial-Indian diplomacy and relations, received a direct appointment from Edward Braddock to the "sole superintendency and management of the affairs of the Six United Nations" and was given command of the desired forty-four-hundred-man provincial force that was being raised to subdue the French garrison at Crown Point.[9] Johnson was, in Braddock's opinion (although he garnished no prior major military experience), "a person particularly qualify'd for [leading the expedition against Crown Point] by his Knowledge of those parts, his great Influence over the Six Nations and the universal opinion they have of him in the Northern Colonies."[10] To assist Johnson and his colonial force in their efforts against the French in Upstate New York, Braddock later appointed Captain William Eyre of the Forty-fourth Regiment of Foot to serve as the army's engineer, quartermaster general and chief of artillery. Eyre would be the only British Regular soldier to serve with Johnson and his provincial force in the summer of 1755.

William Johnson's influence among the Six Nations, and more particularly the Mohawk, would serve a crucial role in the coming campaigns on the New York colonial frontier. It was necessary to muster as much Indian support as possible to fight the French in the wilderness of North America—something at which the French were much more successful than the British at this time in the war. No one was more skilled at gathering intelligence and executing wilderness (irregular) warfare than the North American Indian warrior. Their assistance was key to any army's success, and both Johnson and William Shirley needed their support and numbers. Only one would be able to earn it, though. In a bitter rivalry that ensued between the two men in Albany later that summer, William Johnson always seemed to have the upper hand. Ignorance and politics at the leadership level defined the campaigns of 1755, which were officially set into motion in Alexandria in April. But the adaptation to wilderness warfare and the fighting capability of the colonial provincial soldier against a better-trained enemy would prove to be the real test that ultimately achieved battlefield victories for the British in North America.

2

WILLIAM JOHNSON'S ARMY

t the outbreak of hostilities in 1754, the British military arm in North America was anything but imposing. No British regular line regiments could be found in the colonies, and only seven independent companies from New York and South Carolina were stationed on garrison duty in their respective provinces. Royal regiments recruited in the colonies were not mustered into service until the following year, and the Forty-fourth and Forty-eighth Regiments of Foot with Braddock did not arrive in North America until March 1755. Much of the fighting prior to the formal declaration of war in 1756 between England and France would have to be done by colonial provincial units made up of volunteers and militia conscripts.[11]

Assembling in Albany with Johnson's and Shirley's armies in the summer of 1755 were troops from six different colonies. Connecticut, Massachusetts, New Hampshire, New Jersey, New York and Rhode Island sent men to take part in the upcoming offensive, and each unit brought with it its own personality. According to militia laws of the era in the colonies, the typical age range of each unit would have been somewhere between sixteen and sixty. All able-bodied men in each colony falling in that range who were not exempt (magistrates, teachers, students and so on) were required to serve in their town's militia.[12] However, when recruiting stations were opened in Massachusetts to fill the ranks of the colony's regiments, Governor Shirley issued what were known as "Beating Orders." These orders stipulated that all men taking up arms must be between the ages of eighteen and thirty-five, in acceptable physical shape and no shorter than five feet, four inches tall, healthy and non–Roman Catholic.[13]

The colonies not meeting their suggested quotas for the campaign that were forced to conscript militiamen were much more lenient and accepted a variety of men as long as they could serve.

Eighteenth-century militia and provincial units during the French and Indian War received a wide range of training and were subject to different models of discipline. Many units were drilled in various forms of militia manuals of arms that were in some way or another based on those used by His Majesty's Forces on the European continent. The standard training manual used by the British Regulars was Major General Humphrey Bland's *Treatise of Military Discipline*, originally published in 1727 and modified as warfare evolved during the first half of the century. His work was extremely well regarded by military minds in the colonies, and even Colonel George Washington of the Virginia Regiment ordered his officers to train their men with Bland's manual. Colonel Ephraim Williams of the Third Massachusetts Regiment made sure his men were trained so, in "the Hopes of opposing our Militia (whatever Hearts they may have in their bellies) to Troops who have the advantage of Discipline on their side."[14] Smoothbore muskets of the era required soldiers to be drilled for linear-style combat—in open fields of battle—and the New Englanders and New Yorkers with William Johnson's army certainly would have been familiar with this form of warfare. However, many of the colonists were more adamant about fighting in an irregular style—in broken ranks and behind cover—where their marksmanship skills could be put to the test. The battlefields of North America would be much different than those of Europe and elsewhere in the world. Vast wildernesses took the place of open farm fields, and the army that best utilized terrain and obstacles normally emerged victorious.

SMOOTHBORE MUSKETS AND LINEAR-STYLE WARFARE

To the common individual who does not study military history, the idea of men in the eighteenth century marching shoulder-to-shoulder in perfect lines of battle, moving as closely as possible to their foe, leveling their muskets in concert and unleashing devastating volleys of lead into their opponent's ranks—all the while standing firm and waiting to receive fire from across the field—seems idiotic or even suicidal. However, many do not understand that the concept of linear-style warfare was instituted to fully maximize the effectiveness of the weapons of the era, not to get as many men killed in one's own army as possible.

The standard-issue weapon of all major armies during the colonial expansion era was the flintlock smoothbore musket. For over a century the English army utilized the King's Land Pattern Musket, or "Brown Bess"—a massive .75-caliber smoothbore weapon that packed a punch greater than many of its contemporary counterparts and won a substantial amount of victories for the royal Hanoverian family on battlefields throughout the world. Firing a .69 lead musket ball at a velocity of roughly one thousand feet per second—much slower compared to modern-day firearms—the Brown Bess was a vicious killing machine. However, because the inside of the barrel was completely smooth and not rifled, and due to the fact that the projectile was not conical in shape, the weapon was only accurate at about fifty yards. The inaccuracy of the period's firearms is why armies utilized linear-style tactics on open fields of battle.[15]

To maximize the effectiveness of smoothbore weapons, soldiers marched shoulder-to-shoulder in lines of battle to distances between forty and sixty yards from their enemy before simultaneously leveling their weapons and unleashing a volley of musketry. This concept was far from idiotic, as most believe today. The weapons of the era were not necessarily meant to be fired accurately individually, but en masse. There was a much better chance of hitting a target if several hundred muzzles were aimed in its direction. Compact lines of battle created a literal wall of lead when the soldiers' weapons were discharged.

Every army had its own methods of linear-style combat. During the Seven Years' War the French army tended to deploy its battalions—ranging between 500 and 1,000 men—into four lines, creating a frontage of roughly 162 men or so. Their British adversaries chose to deploy their units two or three ranks deep, which arguably gave them an advantage because they fought with a wider front, producing a longer line of fire.[16]

The professionally trained European soldier of the eighteenth century carrying a flintlock musket could load and fire his weapon three to four times per minute—a tremendous rate for a muzzle-loading weapon. When engaging the enemy in an open field and fighting in the linear style, the idea was to fire two or three volleys into the enemy's ranks, confusing and staggering them. If it was evident that the opponent's men were indeed in a state of panic, the order would be given by officers to fix bayonets. Wielding these long, steel, sword-like weapons at the tip of the musket's muzzle, the battalions would then slowly march (not run) toward the enemy and quite literally sweep them off the field, claiming victory for their respective monarch. If the opposing line chose to stand firm and receive the charge, then hand-to-hand combat would ensue for possession of the battlefield.[17]

Well into the eighteenth century, as smoothbore weapons still served as the predominant arms for the world's militaries, linear-style warfare was constantly utilized in open fields of battle. Eventually, technology outpaced military tactics when the rifle was invented and became the weapon of choice. Effective at much greater distances, rifled muskets made war even bloodier. Still using linear-style tactics in the 1860s, American Civil War armies found this out the hard way. Eventually, lines of battle would become obsolete, and trench warfare became the favored tactic. Even during the French and Indian War it became evident that European linear tactics could not serve the desired purpose in the vast wilderness of North America. A new style of fighting took shape: irregular or guerilla tactics. This method entailed broken ranks moving forward, utilizing terrain features, rocks and trees and anything that could provide cover and shield one's position from the enemy. Many provincial (colonial) and militia units fought in this style, which had been utilized by the Native Americans for centuries. The British even formed light infantry companies to fight in this manner.

Soldiers of the eighteenth century were not idiotic, and they certainly did not have a "death wish" by fighting in compact lines of battle. These were some of the most disciplined and vigorously trained soldiers that the world has ever seen, and they fought with courage and resiliency for king and country. Linear-style combat was a military innovation that was meant to maximize the effectiveness of the era's weapon technology, and it proved efficient on countless battlefields throughout the world, ousting the French from North America and earning an imperial victory for King George II in 1763.

WILLIAM JOHNSON

Responsibility for commanding the provincial army that was tasked with subduing the French at Crown Point fell upon the shoulders of forty-year-old William Johnson. One of the most fascinating and significant personalities in all of colonial history, Johnson possessed little to no military experience when he was given command of the expeditionary forces in April 1755. Born in County Meath, Ireland, in 1715, Johnson came to the colonies in 1738 to manage and oversee a frontier store and fourteen thousand acres of land in the Mohawk River Valley that belonged to his uncle, Royal Navy captain Peter Warren. It was here that Johnson learned the importance of maintaining positive and profitable relations with the Native Americans, specifically the Mohawks, and adopted their culture and customs as part of his own. He took on a mistress, Catherine Weisenberg, who gave him three children—two daughters and a son, John, who was constantly present and consuming alcohol with his father at their Mount Johnson estate. His rise to prominence in regards to Native American diplomacy was so well received that he was appointed to the position of commissary of New York for Indian affairs in 1746 and, two years later, was commissioned a colonel in His Majesty's Forces to oversee the defense of the frontier during King George's War. This was the extent of his military experience. Regardless, William Johnson made friends with the right people as war clouds appeared on the horizon in 1754.[18]

In June 1754, delegates from seven colonies assembled in Albany, New York, to discuss colonial unification against the French and Indian grievances laid out before them by representatives of the Iroquois

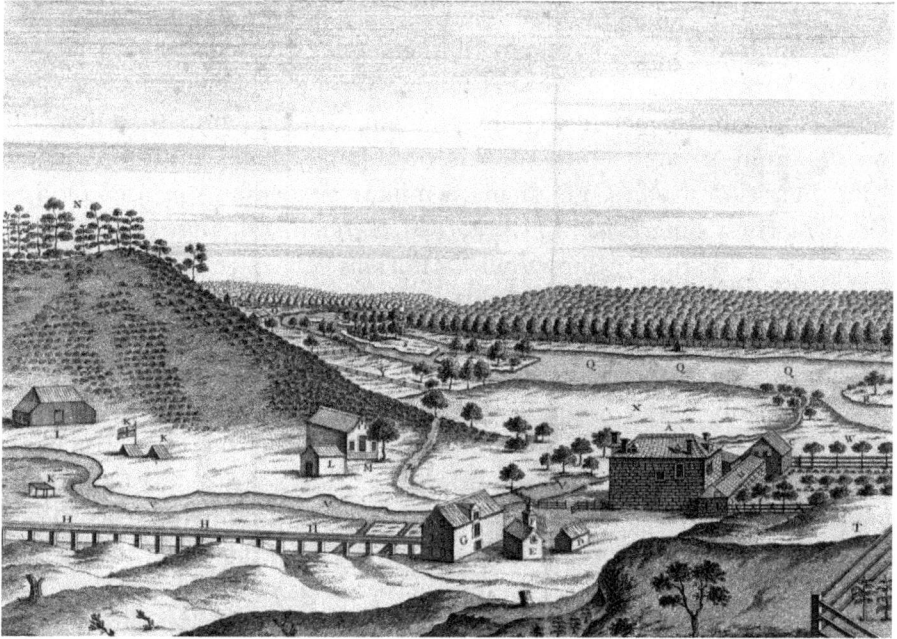

Mount Johnson, William Johnson's Mohawk Valley estate. *Courtesy of New York Public Library Digital Collections.*

Confederacy. Johnson quickly befriended acting New York governor James DeLancey and a young Englishman, Thomas Pownall, the brother of the secretary of the Board of Trade in England. Pownall's connection through his brother, George Montagu Dunk, earl of Halifax, president of the Board of Trade (which was in charge of colonial affairs), obtained Johnson an appointment to superintendent of Indian affairs in the Northern Colonies. The following March, his position and familiarity with the Iroquois earned him his commission as major general in command of the Crown Point expedition.[19]

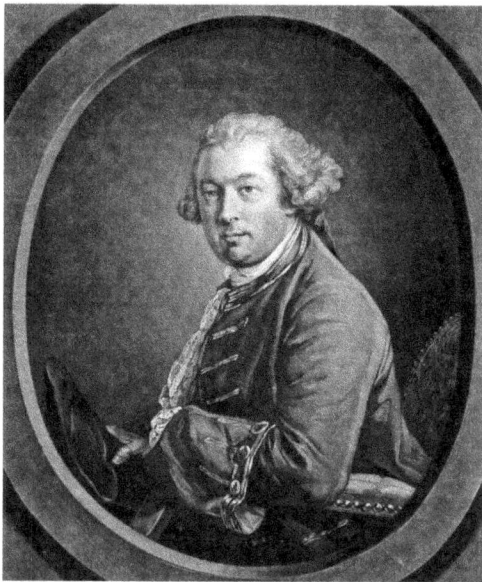

Thomas Pownall. *Courtesy of New York Public Library Digital Collections.*

William Johnson and William Shirley's offensives against the French in New York were to be privately funded. While the colonial assemblies raised troops and armed and equipped them, anything more than that had to come from private sectors. For this, both Johnson and Shirley found aid from their closest allies. Financing a military expedition in the colonies was a business enterprise that put rival merchants against one another in the quest for profit. Shirley was notorious for contracting his friends (as he did during King George's War), and he immediately sought the aid of Pennsylvania governor Robert Morris (who had business contacts in Philadelphia), Morris's nephew Lewis, Thomas Hutchinson of Boston and Peter Van Burgh Livingston. James DeLancey, the most successful merchant in New York City, saw his business rivals on the verge of making a huge profit on the Niagara expedition. He was ecstatic to assist his friend Johnson in supplying the general's campaign in Upstate New York. Thus began the bitter feud between Johnson, Shirley and their contractors that would hinder the success of the northern campaigns of 1755. The two men easily procured the financial support to undertake their expeditions, but what of the Native American support that was to be so crucial toward the armies' success?[20]

As superintendent of Indian affairs, it was Johnson's duty to obtain warriors from the northern tribes to assist his and William Shirley's armies. Essentially going over Johnson's head, Shirley appointed a corrupt merchant named John Henry Lydius to handle the recruiting of native warriors for the Niagara expedition. This could not have been a more terrible decision. Lydius, involved in illegal trading with Canada and the Susquehanna Company deed, which proved to be fraudulent, was never on good terms with the Indians. Furthermore, the effort to win the natives over from Johnson with Lydius proved to be the straw that broke the camel's back between the two generals. Bad blood between the principal army leaders in New York during the summer of 1755 hindered any prospect of success before the campaign season was over. However, before this feud could play itself out, thousands of men from New England, New Jersey and New York were set to assemble in Albany and embark on one of the greatest adventures of their lives.[21]

CONNECTICUT

The 1750 population returns for the colonies listed Connecticut as having over 100,000 white inhabitants. Of that number, roughly a quarter most likely would have been able-bodied men serving in the province's militia. Like its sister New England colony, Massachusetts, Connecticut had an extremely proud military pedigree. Between 1636 and 1638, it had fought a bloody war with the Pequot tribe as part of the Massachusetts Bay Colony. As tensions boiled over in the Ohio River Valley between the colonies and France, Connecticut was ordered to militarize its male populace and raise 1,000 soldiers for the expedition against Crown Point and to assist New York as well, by raising 300 more men to be augmented into the First New York Regiment. The colony succeeded in doing so. The 1,000 men raised for the colony's own military defense would be organized into two provincial regiments, and one of Connecticut's own sons, Phineas Lyman, was appointed by William Shirley as a major general and William Johnson's second-in-command.[22]

Phineas Lyman was born in Durham, Connecticut, in 1716, the son of a weaver. His desire to follow a different route in life than his father and obtain a better education found him enrolled at Yale, from which he graduated in 1738 as a Berkeley scholar—an extremely high honor. Lyman later studied law and relocated to Suffield, Massachusetts; he assisted in admitting the town into the colony of Connecticut. It was in Suffield that he obtained his first experience in a military environment, serving as a major in the town's militia. In 1755, as Connecticut prepared for war against the French, Lyman was given command of the First Connecticut Regiment and appointed by the colony as major general and commander of all the province's forces in March of that year. His rank within New England's provincial forces catapulted him to become Johnson's second-in-command.[23]

Although extremely militaristic and passionate about the English imperial cause—Connecticut supplied King George II with the second-greatest manpower in the colonies during the war—the colony chose to take the route of non-uniformity during the conflict. In 1755, Connecticut's regiments did not sport matching uniforms, like Massachusetts or New Jersey. Instead, most of the men were garbed in their civilian clothing or prewar militia outfits. They also were asked by the Connecticut Assembly to supply their own weapons should they not be able to procure any from storehouses within the colony. The men were issued the proper mess gear, such as wedge tents. Officers were most likely not issued any uniforms, and they, too, wore their militia coats. It was not until 1757 that the officers and men were given uniformed regimentals. Despite the hodgepodge appearance of the Connecticut troops, the two regiments organizing in Albany were made up of tough fighters and brilliant battlefield leaders.[24]

The First Connecticut Regiment was commanded by Phineas Lyman, but during the Battle of Lake George, when the major general was forced to focus on exercising his role as Johnson's second-in-command, the unit was led in the field by the senior field officers. In the ranks of the First Connecticut was a thirty-seven-year-old soldier from Mortlake (present-day Pomfret), Israel Putnam, who would later be appointed a captain and serve in the famous eighteenth-century unit Rogers' Rangers. His career following the French and Indian War would be even more distinguished, serving as a major general in the Continental army. The First Regiment carried roughly four hundred men throughout the campaign of 1755 and, along with the Second Connecticut, fought valiantly at Lake George.[25]

The second regiment that the colony mustered for service was commanded by Colonel Elizur Goodrich. Not much is known about Goodrich and his upbringing other than that he was born in Wethersfield in 1693 and left the service in 1756. His second-in-command was Lieutenant Colonel Nathan Whiting of Windham, Connecticut. Born on May 4, 1724, Whiting was the son of a reverend and a direct descendant of William Bradford, governor of Plymouth Colony and signer of the Mayflower

Compact. Whiting graduated from Yale in 1743 and, two years later, served alongside many other men destined for greatness in the French and Indian War as part of the Louisbourg expedition during King George's War. He so distinguished himself during the great colonial victory over the French that he was commissioned a lieutenant in the British army—a feat not accomplished by many, especially by a New Englander in his early twenties. At age thirty-one in the spring and summer of 1755, Whiting was one of Johnson's youngest field officers.[26]

Although Goodrich technically commanded the regiment, it seems as if Whiting led the unit in the field and made the command his own via motivation and leadership. Assembling in New Haven in May 1755 before making their way to Albany, the men of the Second Connecticut Regiment took a knee and listened to a very upbeat and inspirational sermon by Reverend Isaac Stiles entitled "The Character and Duty of Souldiers [sic]." The reverend urged the Connecticut men to "file off the rust of their firelocks" and to "attend to the several beats of that great warlike instrument the drum, and to the language of that shrill high-sounding trumpet, that noble, reviving and animated sound." Nearly presenting the men with a divine premonition, he spoke of the enemy "lying slain on the battle field with battered arms, bleeding sculls [sic] and cloven trunks," while Whiting and his men, "the good souldiers of Jesus Christ were all the while shining with all the beauty and luster that inward sanctity and outward charms lend to the hero's look." Connecticut was going to war.[27]

MASSACHUSETTS

Massachusetts, of all of His Majesty King George II's colonies in North America, was by far the most militaristic. Between fighting wars against various Native American tribes throughout the colony and conducting campaigns against the French during the previous colonial conflicts, Massachusetts was always willing to place its own sons on the frontlines. William Shirley had initially recommended to Johnson that four thousand men be recruited and mustered into service to help subdue the French garrison at Crown Point and that Massachusetts would send twelve hundred. However, by late May 1755, the Bay Colony had managed to send fifteen hundred provincials to Albany, where the expeditionary force was assembling.[28]

Mustering at Albany in the spring of 1755 were three regiments of Massachusetts provincial soldiers—designated accordingly as the First, Second and Third Regiments and commanded, respectively, by Colonels Timothy Ruggles, Moses Titcomb and Ephraim Williams. Each unit was made up of ten companies of fifty men each and at full strength could put five hundred soldiers into the field. Desertions and sickness caused these numbers to fluctuate throughout the campaign, but Massachusetts—sticking to its prideful militaristic culture—still supplied William Johnson's army with the most fighting men.

Besides the Jersey Blues, Massachusetts's provincial units were the best-equipped and best-uniformed men belonging to the armies assembling at Albany in June–July 1755. It was one of the wealthiest colonies in North America, and the Massachusetts Assembly was able to provide its troops with a higher quality of arms and accoutrements. Each man was issued a King's Land Pattern Musket with a bayonet, the proper tools for maintaining and repairing their firelocks, a cartridge box and a bullet bag for ammunition, as well as a powder horn. For close-quarter combat the men carried hatchets or swords. Unlike many of the other New England regiments, Massachusetts's enlisted men displayed uniformity by receiving blue regimentals with red lapels, red breeches and waistcoat, probably blue stockings and a cocked hat. Officer uniforms varied depending on rank.

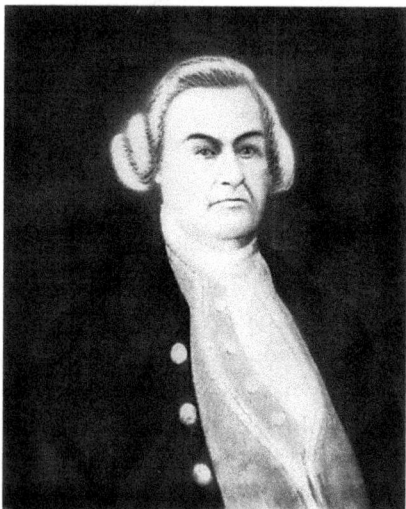

Colonel Timothy Ruggles, First Massachusetts Regiment. *From* The Papers of Sir William Johnson, *vol. 2 (Albany, 1921).*

Ensigns, lieutenants and captains wore the enlisted blue, but with scarlet facing opposed to red and gold lacing on their waistcoats and hats. Majors, lieutenant colonels, colonels and generals wore red coats without lapels or cuffs. They also utilized gold lacings on their waistcoats and tricorn hats. At the Battle of Lake George in September 1755, the three Massachusetts regiments would have definitely been the easiest to distinguish from the rest of William Johnson's army.[29]

Massachusetts's First Provincial Regiment was commanded by forty-three-year-old Colonel Timothy Ruggles and hailed from the central and southern regions of the colony. His second-in-command was Lieutenant Colonel Thomas Gilbert. Ruggles, born in Rochester, Massachusetts, in 1711, graduated from Harvard in 1732 and proceeded to practice law in his hometown as well as representing it as a member of the provincial assembly. Well regarded by his peers and especially men with influence in colonial affairs, he was appointed colonel of the First Massachusetts Regiment and mustered into the provincial service in March 1755. His success as a military leader during the French and Indian War catapulted him to the rank of brigadier general in the Massachusetts Provincial Forces.[30]

The Second Massachusetts Provincial Regiment was led during the summer of 1755 by Colonel Moses Titcomb, a veteran of King George's War and the New England expedition against the French stronghold Fortress Louisbourg in 1745. Titcomb was, according to Newbury, Massachusetts pastor John Lowell, "a Gentleman well known, and highly esteemed, thro' this Country, for his military Accomplishments." The colonel's "Service for His King and Country [during King George's War] was greatly detrimental to his private Fortune, yet no sooner was he again called for by them, than his Regard for the public Welfare prevailed over all Considerations of private Interest and personal Hazard, and he readily took the Field at the Head of a Regiment." Titcomb would take with him to Albany over four hundred men from the eastern sections of the colony—many from Boston. His second-in-command was Lieutenant Colonel Jonathan Bagley.[31]

The third of Massachusetts's regiments to be mustered into service for the Crown Point expedition belonged to Colonel Ephraim Williams and consisted of men from the western reaches of the colony. As delegates from Massachusetts and six other colonies met in Albany to discuss unification and Native American affairs, steps were being taken to militarize New England once again. Commissions were handed out to some of the colony's prominent individuals who possessed some form of military experience as war clouds gathered. One of the men to receive a commission was Ephraim Williams, a

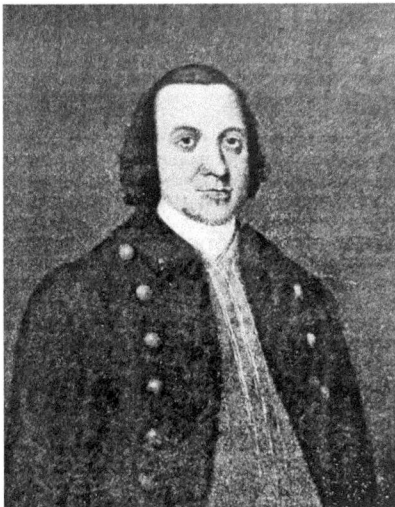

Colonel Moses Titcomb, Second Massachusetts Regiment. *Courtesy of Library of Congress.*

native of Stockbridge and veteran of King George's War and battles against the Indians throughout the colony.[32]

Born in 1715 in Newton, Massachusetts, Ephraim Williams Jr. was the son of Ephraim and Elizabeth Williams. From one of the more prominent families in early eighteenth-century Massachusetts, Williams was destined to earn an education, live a wealthy life and have a powerful role in his colony's military or judicial system. He chose to live the life of a soldier and received a captain's commission in 1745. He was later garrisoned at Fort Massachusetts along the Hoosic River to guard the colonial frontier against French and Indian raids during King George's War (1744–48), the title given to the North American theater of Europe's much larger War of Austrian Succession then being waged. In August 1746, the fort's garrison was besieged and eventually surrendered to a large body of French and Indians. Luckily for Williams and his younger brother Thomas, who was also serving on duty there, the two were absent on personal or professional business during the siege and did not have to make the journey to Quebec with the rest of the captured garrison. The fort was later rebuilt, and again Williams was assigned to command it. Besides taking part in minor skirmishes with enemy raiding parties along the frontier, Ephraim did not see any large-scale combat before the Treaty of Aix-la-Chappelle was signed in 1748, ending the war. Regardless of this, as warfare between England and France once again broke out in North America less than a decade later, Williams, part of a well-respected family and holding experience as a captain, was given a commission as a major by the Massachusetts Assembly to once again help subdue the Indians in the western part of the colony as it prepared for another war.[33]

The following spring, in 1755, William Shirley presented Williams with a provincial commission as a colonel to lead one of the regiments set to be raised for the expedition against Crown Point. An avid student of military history and an admirer of Oliver Cromwell, the new colonel would instill a great deal of discipline into his unit's training, sticking firmly to the ideas of Major General Humphrey Bland. His men would look and fight like soldiers, and so would he. It is said that before going into battle, Williams would dress down to the attire of a common soldier and even exchange his saber for a musket in order to appear less of a target to the enemy. However, when in camp and attending dinners or special duties, the colonel sported a very flamboyant scarlet coat, leather breeches with silver buttons, linen stockings, silk handkerchiefs, a wig and a black cockade hat. He resembled a gentlemen and a professional officer. The men respected him, and he respected their devotion to the cause. His admiration of William Johnson was something to be desired, though. In his eyes the commanding general greatly lacked the experience necessary to lead such an army and expedition. Regardless, Williams did his duty and vowed to defend his home from the encroaching French and Indians.[34]

Serving as his second-in-command was Lieutenant Colonel Seth Pomeroy of Northampton, Massachusetts. Forty-nine years old in the summer of 1755, Pomeroy was also a veteran of King George's War. In 1745, William Shirley planned an expedition to capture the French stronghold of Louisbourg on Nova Scotia's Cape Breton Island. In April of that year a taskforce of forty-three hundred New England volunteers besieged the fortress and forced its capitulation a month and a half later. Pomeroy held the rank of major of Massachusetts provincials and was present during the surrender. His experience obtained during the Louisbourg expedition, as well as the help of some respected colleagues, earned him a commission with the Third Massachusetts Regiment on March 29, 1755. He arrived in Albany during the first week of July.[35]

NEW HAMPSHIRE

In 1755, as the New England colonies were raising men for the Crown Point Expedition, New Hampshire was asked to join the war effort by enlisting five hundred provincials for military service, or one full regiment. That unit became the First New Hampshire Regiment and was commanded by fifty-one-year-old Colonel Joseph Blanchard of Dunstable. Although the colony had been forced to militarize a decade prior during King George's War to defend its settlements from French-allied Indians, at the outbreak of the French and Indian War the province's military forces were in bad shape. The men conscripted or enlisting within the ranks of Blanchard's provincials were forced to provide themselves with nearly all of their own arms and equipment—albeit some bounties were distributed upon joining in order for the men to purchase the necessary materials. They carried their personal firearms and wore civilian clothing. It was not until 1757 when the New Hampshire men were issued some sort of regimental uniform. They were ill-trained soldiers from all walks of life and bore the brunt of the army's poor provisioning. Because the regiment was forced to take a much longer and tenuous route in order to reach Johnson's staging area for the campaign, it did not arrive in Albany until August 11 and 12, 1755. Their role in the Battle

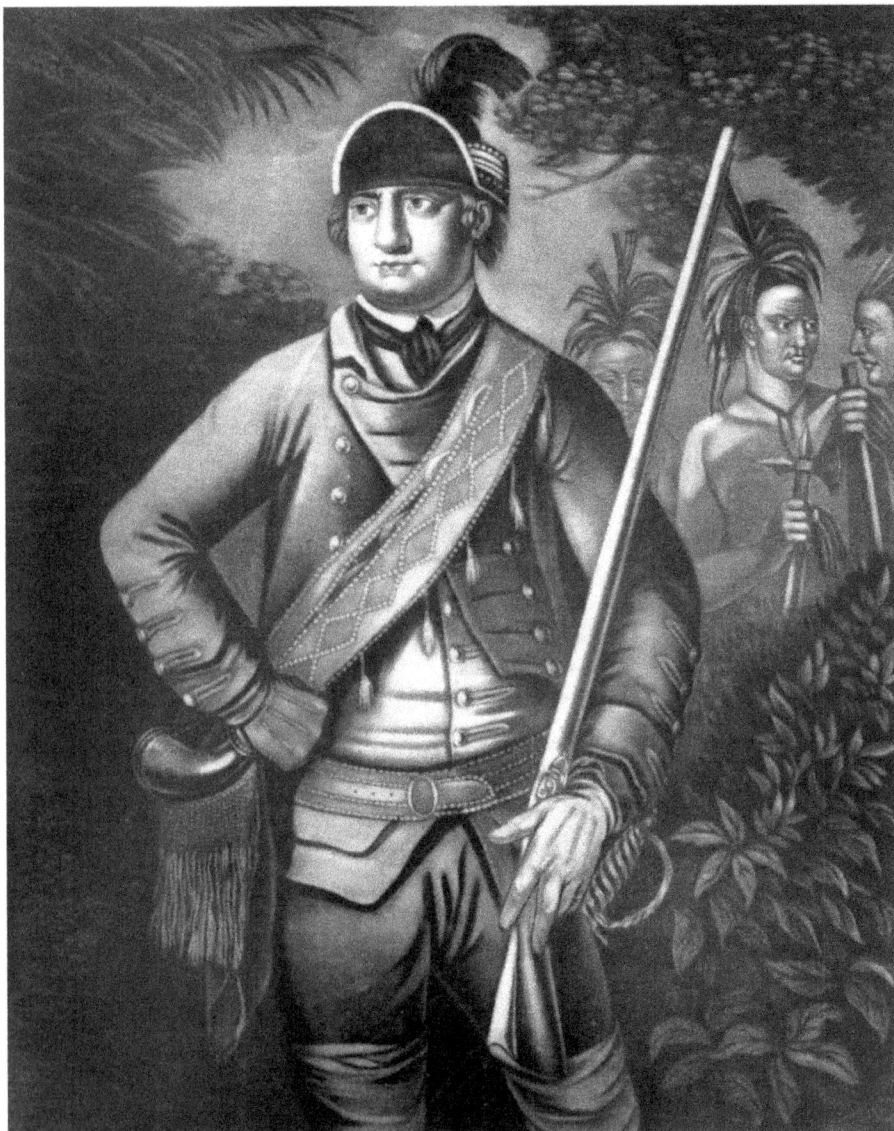

Robert Rogers. *Courtesy of New York Public Library Digital Collections.*

of Lake George was minimal because they were left behind at Fort Lyman (Edward), fourteen miles south of Lake George. But their presence as a last line of defense should the French push toward Albany was crucial. Present with the First New Hampshire Regiment at Fort Lyman was a company of rangers. Among its ranks were Robert Rogers—future commanding officer of Rogers' Rangers and author of a military doctrine, *Rules of Ranging*—and another man destined for fame and glory in the American Revolutionary War, John Stark.[36]

NEW JERSEY

Of all the provincial units assembling at Albany during June–August 1755, none was better armed or equipped than Colonel Peter Schuyler's First New Jersey Regiment. Garbed in blue regimental coats with red facings and blue or buckskin breeches, the unit had been given the nickname "Jersey Blues" during King George's War the previous decade. The unit was fully equipped with camp gear and accoutrements and wielded Dutch muskets that were held in surplus. The locks constantly broke, the hammers were too soft and no spark could be ignited when struck by the cock. Though the quality of their firelocks left the men complaining throughout the war, they still sported the most complete and professional-looking uniforms.[37]

The regiment could trace its lineage to the seventeenth century and fought in nearly every major battle of the French and Indian War. So proud was New Jersey of its Blues that in 1758 a company of grenadiers was raised for service in the regiment. In July of the previous year, the Jersey Blues were garrisoned at Fort William Henry and embarked on a reconnaissance trip up Lake George with the goal of locating the whereabouts of the French and their Indian allies. The large party was ambushed at Sabbath Day Point and suffered a staggering 260 casualties. However, in 1755, the horror and reality of combat lay far in the future for the Jersey Blues as they assembled in Albany. Originally assigned to travel north to Crown Point with Johnson's expeditionary force, fate had other plans for the five hundred men from New Jersey—and so did William Shirley.

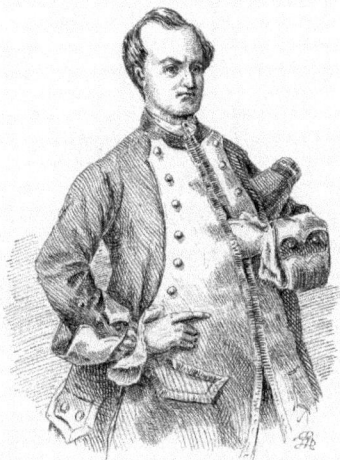

Colonel Peter Schuyler, First New Jersey "Jersey Blues" Regiment. *Courtesy of New York Public Library Digital Collections.*

Concerned that the Royal Regiments would need more manpower in order to subdue the French at Fort Niagara, Shirley asserted his power as His Majesty's Forces second-in-command in North America and stripped Johnson of the Blues, sending them to Fort Oswego along the southeastern shore of Lake Ontario. The following year, Peter Schuyler and his men would meet disaster at the hands of the Marquis de Montcalm.[38]

NEW YORK

In May 1755, the New York Assembly passed an act that called for the raising of eight hundred provincial troops to assist its neighboring colonies against the encroaching French and their Indian allies. It was also determined by the assembly to raise a sum of £10,000 toward the effort in "one or more forts [near] Crown-Point, within his Majesty's Dominions." To help assist in the defense of the colony against its immediate threat astride Lake Champlain, the assembly also reached out to Connecticut for five hundred more men, who could be augmented into New York's provincial ranks. Already raising one thousand men for its own two regiments, the Connecticut Assembly was not confident that it could entice another five hundred to enlist—especially to fight for another colony. The assembly eventually consented and granted New York representative Oliver DeLancey "liberty for inlisting three compleat companies of one hundred effective men each, officers included . . . to be commanded by officers that may be nominated by the Assembly of this Colony [Connecticut]." Under that final provision, the assembly nominated twenty-eight-year-old Yale graduate Eleazer Fitch of Lebanon, Connecticut, as a major in the New York regiment. Fitch was to serve as the unit's secondary commanding officer; William Johnson was commissioned as the regiment's colonel, but the rank given to him, major general, would not allow him to serve as the unit's commanding field officer. Instead, on May 3, when the regiment was officially ordered to be raised, William Cockcroft was made its acting colonel.[39]

Eleazer Fitch was born in Lebanon on August 29, 1726, and graduated from Yale in 1743, becoming a lawyer shortly thereafter. After marrying three years later he moved to Windham, where he became well known as a public servant. In May the Connecticut Assembly nominated him as major of the First New York Regiment, and he made his way to Albany with the three hundred men of his home colony who would augment the unit.

Because the colony of New York took on the "pay and encouragements" of the Connecticut men, they probably would have been clothed and equipped in the same manner as Governor DeLancey's provincials. The New Yorkers were clothed in blue regimentals with red facings and blue waistcoats worn underneath—all linen, most likely. They sported felt hats and blue breeches or trousers when performing fatigue duties. The men were supplied with full mess equipment and wielded King's Land Pattern Muskets or Dutch Muskets like the Jersey Blues (depending on what was available). If arms were scarce, they were given bounties upon enlistment to purchase their own firelocks. In 1755, the well-equipped New Yorkers were fighting to defend their families and homes in the wilderness of their own colony's frontier.[40]

Rhode Island

The colony of Rhode Island was ecstatic at the opportunities presented as a result of war between England and France. The conflict would enhance the need for privateering and risky trade business for civilian and military supplies and give the colony a chance to secure its shoreline and ports, which for decades had been under attack by raiding parties of French sailors. William Shirley ordered the tiny seashore colony to raise four hundred men for the Crown Point expedition and succeeded in doing so by mustering into service four companies, which together formed the First Rhode Island Regiment. The provincial unit was commanded by Lieutenant Colonel Edward Cole, about whom there is not much known. The men were not issued regimental uniforms; again, like many of the other soldiers with Johnson's army, they sported their prewar militia garb or civilian wear. They were issued a bounty of fifteen pounds with which to purchase a functioning firelock for the expedition. The four hundred men of Lieutenant Colonel Cole's Rhode Island Regiment played a pivotal role in the morning engagement at the Battle of Lake George.[41]

Native Americans

One of the most important pieces of any French and Indian War army was the Native American warriors allied with it. Their superb skills as

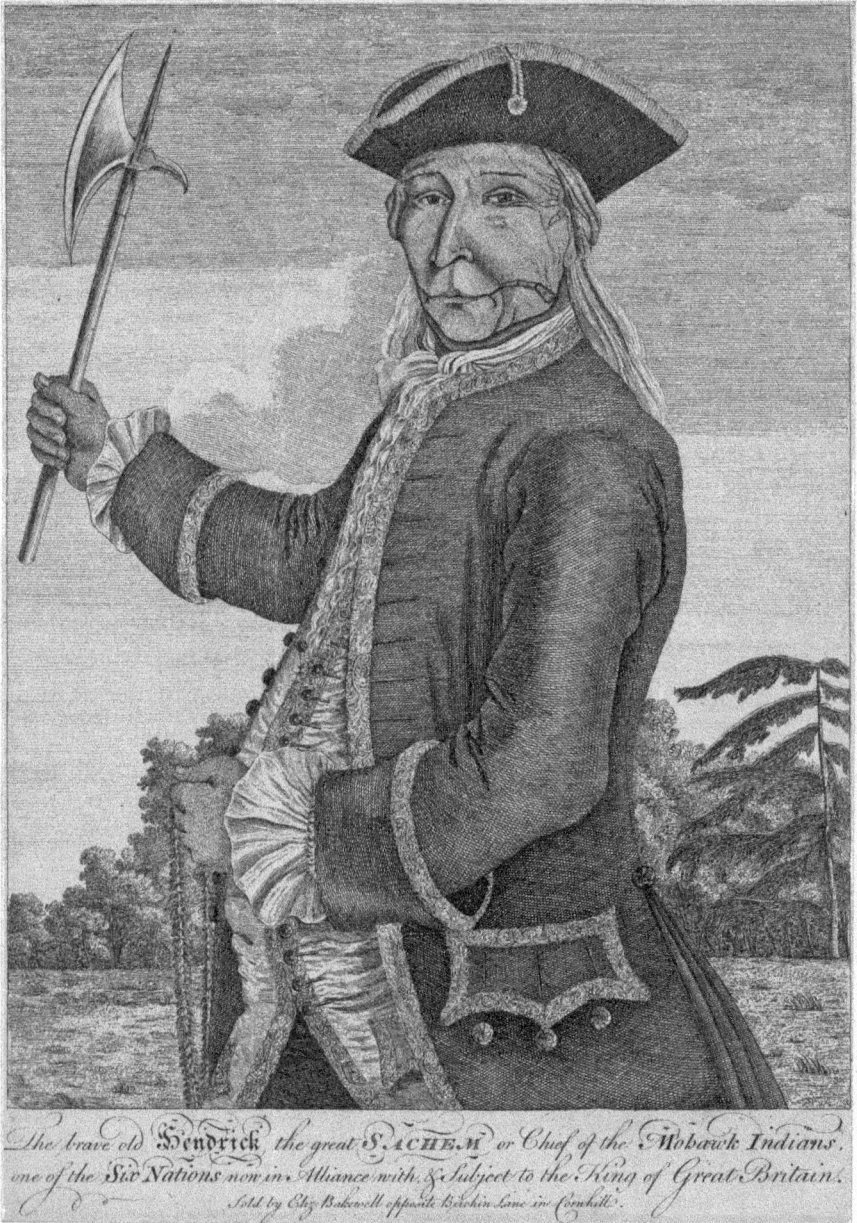

Theyanoguin, Mohawk sachem known to the English as King Hendrick. *Courtesy of New York Public Library Digital Collections.*

irregular fighters and for gathering intelligence made them incredibly sought after when military campaigns were taking shape. The Crown Point Expedition was no exception to this, as William Johnson and William Shirley maneuvered to obtain the support of the Iroquois.

As superintendent of Indian affairs, it was Johnson's duty to rally the natives to England's cause and secure their assistance in both his and Shirley's armies. On June 21, 1755, Johnson called for a meeting with members of the Six Nations to be held at his Mohawk Valley estate. Over one thousand men, women and children attended the meeting. For the next two weeks

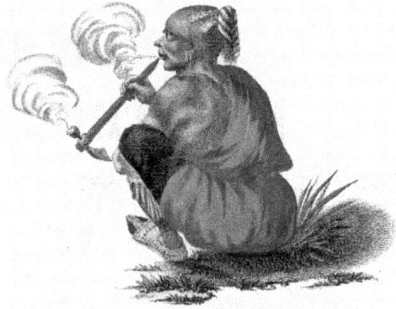

Habit of a Mohawk one of the Six Nations.

A Mohawk Indian. *Courtesy of New York Public Library Digital Collections.*

the conference consisted of various ceremonies, speeches and trading of symbolic items and goods. Johnson's principal allies were the Mohawks. He was accustomed to their traditions and teachings, and they viewed him as their chief defender against fraudulent land deals and corruption. He valued the Mohawks' way of life and was determined to have them remain loyal to England during the escalating conflict against France.[42]

One of Johnson's closets friends and assistants during the Mount Johnson conference was a sachem in his early sixties, Theyanoguin, known to the English as King Hendrick. A Mohegan by birth, Hendrick was adopted by the Mohawks and became a respected diplomat and warrior. He even traveled to London in 1740 and paid a visit to King George II. At the June–July conference along the Mohawk River, he was able to gather three hundred of his warriors to accompany Johnson's army.[43]

BARON DE DIESKAU
AND THE FRENCH ARMY

*F*rance's military arm in North America was anything but spectacular in comparison to what the British sent to North America in 1758. However, three years prior, at the outbreak of hostilities between the two European powers, France could boast that the number of soldiers it could put in the field in North America was equal to or even greater than its adversary's. The forces of New France comprised French Regulars (*troupe de terre*), Colonial Marines (Compagnies Franches de la Marine or Troupes de la Marine), Canadian militia (*malice*) and Native Americans. All in all, King Louis XV could muster over twenty thousand men in 1755 to defend France's colonial possessions in Nova Scotia, Canada, and down the Mississippi River to Louisiana. This was quite a difficult task with a population of only fifty-five thousand in New France, compared to that of over a million in the British colonies. Manpower was never to be in France's favor once King George II and William Pitt determined to make the conquest of North America a top priority several years later. However, in 1754–1755, the forces of New France had their best opportunity to gain a crushing military victory against England before any official war was even declared.[44]

Before the arrival of Jean-Armand, Baron de Dieskau and his roughly three thousand French Regulars of the Regiments of Artois, Béarn, Bourgoyne, Guyenne, Languedoc and La Reine, the only men tasked with combatting the "encroaching" British in North America were the Marines, militia and Native Americans of Canada, the Ohio River Valley and the Great Lakes. Having to fight off only small provincial companies and two

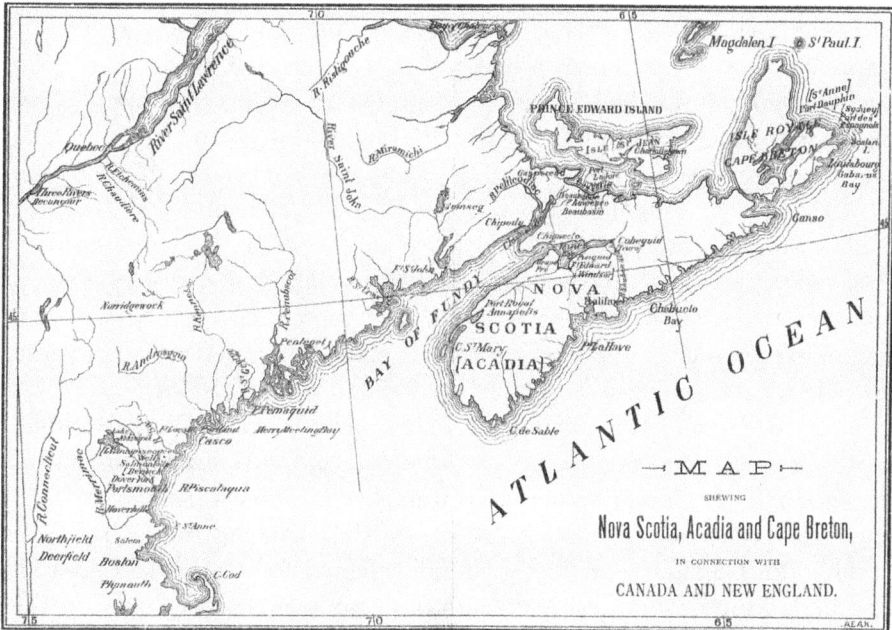

Map of eastern New France and Nova Scotia. *From* The History of Canada, *vol. 3 (Toronto, 1889).*

regiments of British Regulars throughout the first year of the conflict, the soldiers of New France fared very well and proved themselves superior irregular warfare tacticians. Like the English colonies to the south, Canada relied heavily on militia to defend its frontier and interior. All able-bodied men between the ages of sixteen and sixty were required to serve in the militia, unless of course they were serving in the Troupes de la Marine. The men standing within the ranks of the Colonial Marines were recruited in France and sent to Canada under an eight-year term of service. When their enlistments were up, they were encouraged to stay and settle in New France. Officers were usually of a higher class and held some family connection to the colonial forces. The Troupes de la Marine was under the direct control of the Ministry of the Navy and therefore was not commanded by regular French officers sent to the colonies. By 1750 there were thirty companies of fifty Marines each—roughly fifteen hundred men. The regulars arriving in New France during the spring of 1755 took to the field under a *maréchal de camp*, fighting as their English counterparts—in the linear style.[45]

More than a month before Edward Braddock even met with the royal governors in Alexandria, Virginia, to lay out the plans for the upcoming campaign, France was taking the necessary measures to ensure that its colonial possessions in North America would be secure. On March 1, 1755, Jean-Arman, Baron de Dieskau, was appointed to the command of six battalions of regular troops being sent to Canada. Fifty-four years old and a veteran of multiple European conflicts, Dieskau was a protégé of the Comte de Saxe, serving as his aide-de-camp at the age of nineteen. During the War of Austrian Succession, he led cavalry at the Battle of Fontenoy and was afterward made a full major general and the military governor of Brest, a major French naval base. His previously held military posts and exposure to the military genius of the Comte de Saxe made him a perfect candidate to lead the regulars being sent to North America.[46]

Two months after being appointed to his new command, Dieskau and the newly assigned governor-general of New France, Pierre Francois, Marquis de Vaudreuil de Cavagnal, departed from Brest onboard the seventy-four-gun *L'Esperance* alongside fifteen men-of-war ships carrying the six battalions destined for Canada. The fleet was under the watchful eye of Admiral Du Bois de la Motte, who was tasked with protecting and successfully escorting two of France's most important individuals. He would have to combat the elements as well as any English ships determined to impede the voyage.[47]

The Marquis de Vaudreuil, serving as governor-general, was the overseer of all military affairs in New France. Because of this, Dieskau was his subordinate and had to confer with him on all military matters. Vaudreuil held direct authority over all Troupes de la Marine and militia, while Dieskau commanded the regular troops. All decisions for the upcoming campaign against the English would be made by Vaudreuil. Dieskau's direct orders from the court of Louis XV regarding his relationship with the governor-general were as follows:

> *The manner in which Baron de Dieskau is to conduct himself towards the Governor-General of Canada, to whom the nature of his commission renders him necessarily subordinate, remains to be disposed of. The Governor will leave to him all the details of the command, discipline, police and interior service of the land forces, but Baron de Dieskau will be bound, nevertheless, to render him an account thereof, in order that the Governor-General be acquainted with their strength, situation, and, generally, with all that can contribute to put him in possession of the advantage he may derive therefrom, for the success of the operations he shall have to set on foot.*
>
> *It is therefore indispensable that the Baron de Dieskau maintain the best understanding with the Governor-General, acting in concert in*

all things, and that he avoid, as much as possible, all separation from
him, unless the Governor-General put him in charge of some expedition
requiring his presence . . .

Should the Governor-General think proper to assemble a council of
war for the purpose of concerting the operations of the campaign, he will
invite to it, without hesitation, Baron de Dieskau. . . . But whether the
Governor-General take the advice of the council of war or content himself
with conferring in private with Baron de Dieskau, or decide independently
without any previous communication, the said Baron shall be bound to
obey the orders and instructions he shall give him, either for marching
detachments or heading an expedition himself, and he will not be at liberty
to make any change in what shall be prescribed to him, only so far as the
Governor-General will have left him free so to do, or in urgent and unforeseen
circumstances, which shall be reported to him on the spot. Said Governor-
General shall be at liberty to send new orders pending the expedition, and
to repair, should he desire, to the spot, to assume the chief command and
terminate what will have been commenced.[48]

Dieskau, holding the rank of *maréchal de camp*, must have felt that he was in an awkward position and was to have his hands bound during the upcoming campaign. Maintaining a respectable relationship with the governor-general was crucial to ultimate success against the British in North America. Vaudreuil would be calling all of the shots.

The son of a former governor-general in Canada, Vaudreuil was born in Quebec in 1698. His father had come from Languedoc to Canada as an officer in the Troupes de la Marine before being appointed to his post as governor in 1703. Securing a commission in the colonial forces for his son, Vaudreuil served as an officer for some twenty years before journeying to Europe after holding the post of Louisiana's governor. Harboring strong connections in Paris, Vaudreuil was appointed governor-general of New France on April 1, 1755 (the first Canadian to hold the office) and replaced the ailing Marquis de Duquesne. "With a class of writers," according to the 1889 *The History of Canada*, "no governor is spoken of with greater admiration, and they place his name in prominence for capacity and energy. He had the misfortune to be the last French governor-general; and there are many who even maintain that it was only because his policy was not followed, that the province was lost to France." England's conquest of Canada was far away in 1755, however. Vaudreuil's first task as governor-general was to make sure King George II's colonial claims remained along the eastern seaboard.[49]

Dieskau and Vaudreuil's voyage to North America was to take roughly four weeks. The elements made the trip extremely difficult, as gale-force winds, heavy fog and icebergs proved to be vicious obstacles for the squadron. Another more serious impediment lurked ahead. Unbeknownst to the men of la Motte's crew, English spies in France had reported to London that the fleet was sailing from Brest with a destination of North America. In Nova Scotia, Admiral Edward Boscawen received orders from the cabinet to set sail and "fall upon [and] prevent French ships from going into or landing any forces on the continent of North America." Boscawen, a thirty-year veteran in His Majesty's service, was given an unenviable task. Not only was it his duty to prevent the French from strengthening their military might in New France, but he was also tasked with attacking a nation that England was not officially at war with. If the fighting at Jumonville Glen and Fort Necessity had not done so the year prior, this act of war was to serve as the final straw.[50]

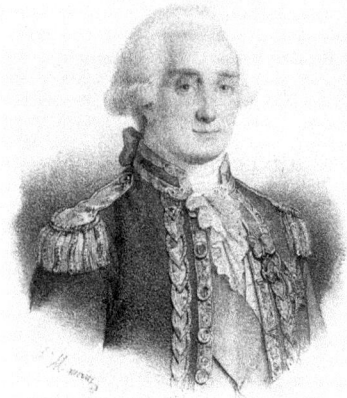

Pierre Francois, Marquis de Vaudreuil de Cavagnal, Governor-General of New France. *Courtesy of New York Public Library Digital Collections.*

On June 7, word reached Captain Richard Howe (brother of George and William and destined for fame during the Revolutionary War) of the *Dunkirk* that fishermen had spotted French vessels carrying a large quantity of soldiers west. Howe set out in pursuit, but bad weather prevented his crew from catching up with the French ships. Boscawen and the rest of the English squadron rendezvoused with Howe's ship leading the van and continued the chase the following day. Maneuvering close enough to the French ships in order for their colors to be in view, Boscawen ordered the flag of France to be raised. The next day, June 9, 1755, the French ships began signaling to Boscawen, only to receive in return a suspicious reply that made them realize their mistake. They immediately hightailed it away, but one of the vessels, *L'Alcide*, was intercepted by Richard Howe and the *Dunkirk*. Attempting to invoke a sea battle between the two peaceful nations, Howe and *L'Alcide*'s captain, Toussaint Hocquart, began exchanging pleasantries as the two men awaited for Boscawen to arrive and assess the situation. However, under strict orders to prevent the French ships from reaching North America even if they had to be destroyed in doing so, Boscawen ordered his men-of-war to engage Hocquart and two other vessels with him. The English ship let loose a devastating broadside and immediately forced *L'Alcide* to surrender. Soon after, the *Lys* submitted to Boscawen's squadron as well, and a total of eight companies of infantry now belonged to the English as prisoners. The brief encounter was a British victory nonetheless. But unbeknownst until after the fight, the three French ships were merely stragglers that had fallen behind the rest of la Motte's squadron. The remaining ships and seventy companies of French regular troops were closing in on their destination: Quebec. There was no denying that what had occurred under Boscawen's command was an act of war; his orders from London had reminded him to not fear the repercussions. Following yet another act of war committed by England during a time of peace, Baron de Dieskau, Vaudreuil and the three thousand regulars of four different regiments were ready to respond and take back what Louis XV believed was rightfully his.[51]

On June 23, the vessels finally arrived in Quebec, and the men disembarked from their ships after being at sea for nearly two months—a much longer voyage than was originally anticipated. Vaudreuil's first order of business was to begin rallying the Canadians to his cause and muster the support of the northwestern Indians. At the beginning of July, Vaudreuil moved himself to Montreal and ordered farmers to Quebec in order to harvest the crops of those men who were assembling as part of the militia that was to participate in the summer's military campaign. The main objective for the French in North America that year was going to be Fort Oswego aside Lake Ontario. The regiments of Béarn and Guyenne were ordered to Fort Frontenac at the northeastern corner of the lake, while Dieskau and the regiments of Languedoc and La Reine moved to Fort Niagara. Both of these fortifications were to be used as staging areas for a push against the English at Oswego. Vaudreuil worked to obtain the support of

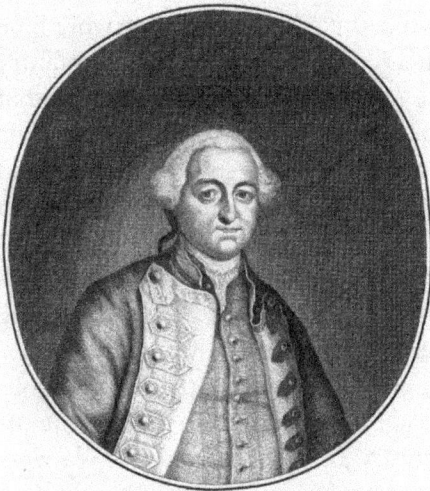

Admiral Edward Boscawen. *Courtesy of New York Public Library Digital Collections.*

Canadian militia and Native Americans as Dieskau and his regulars began the first phase of the campaign.[52]

The French regular army in 1755 was composed of roughly 84 regiments and 172 battalions. Each battalion contained 13 companies of about 40 men each. The battalions of the regiments of Artois and Bourgoyne landed at the fortress of Louisbourg on Cape Breton Island, while the other four went to Quebec. These men were all recruited and organized within their respective provinces and were led by officers of nobility, many of who had only received their prestige through long-term service in His Most Christian Majesty's forces. The enlistment term for a typical man serving in the French army (he was required to be Roman Catholic) was between six to eight years. The military provided each soldier with clothing, food, shelter and a steady pay but did not offer much opportunity for advancement if he was a member of the lower class. They were trained in the linear style in order to meet their foe in the open fields of Europe and carried a .69 Model 1728 smoothbore musket, known as the "Charleville" because of an armory where some were manufactured. Extremely deadly and efficient, the Charleville was much easier to disassemble that its Brown Bess counterpart because it was designed with a three-band system that held the barrel in place, as opposed to the pin system that the British weapons utilized. Each French regular soldier was garbed in a gray-white coat with various facing colors and waistcoats to distinguish the regiments from one another. As for the units that would fight at Lake George in 1755, the Regiment of Languedoc sported red cuffs and a red waistcoat, while the men of La Reine wore blue waistcoats to match the blue cuffs on their coats. When the French infantry arrived in North America in the middle of 1755, they quickly realized that the environment and terrain were much different than that in their home country. Adapting to the vast wilderness and irregular style of warfare was a necessity that took some time. They were also introduced to the North American Indian.[53]

At the outbreak of hostilities in the Ohio River Valley in 1754, the French held the upper hand in Native American relations. Easy access to trading gave them an advantage because many of the eastern woodland tribes' villages were located in proximity to Canada. These were the First Nations of the St. Lawrence River Valley; they had been trading with the inhabitants of New France since the seventeenth century. In 1755, six hundred warriors of four different nations agreed to accompany Dieskau's army. Over half of this contingent was made up of members of the Caughnawagas from the missions of Sault St. Louis and of the Lake of the Two Mountains. Canadian

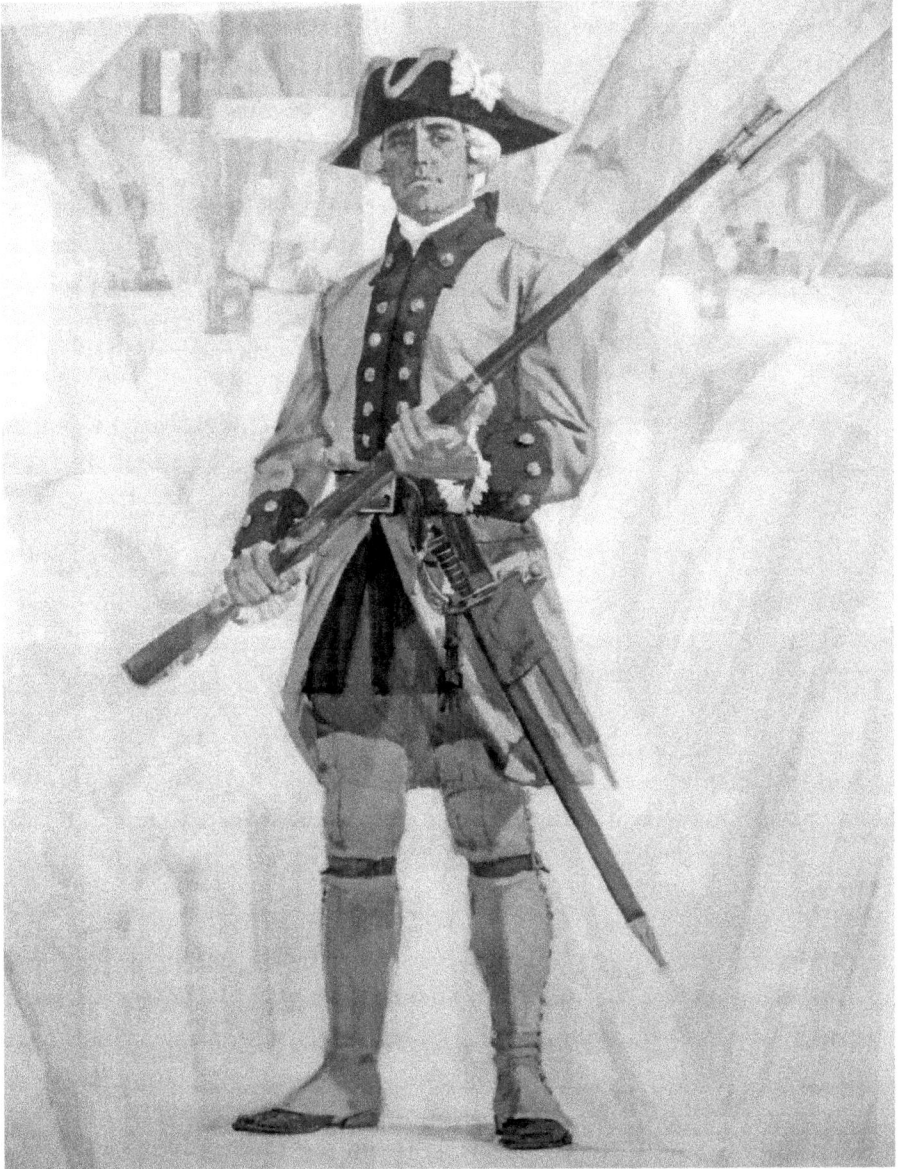

A soldier of the Regiment de Languedoc. *Painting by Charny.*

Iroquois and cousins to the English Mohawks, Dieskau worried about their devotion to the French cause. "Before quitting Montreal," he wrote in his report following the Battle of Lake George, "I had already various reasons for suspecting the fidelity of the domiciliated Iroquois . . . composing half of the

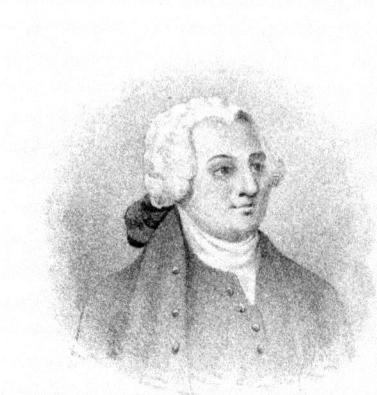

ROBERT DINWIDDIE
Governor of Virginia.

Robert Dinwiddie, royal governor of Virginia. *Courtesy of New York Public Library Digital Collections.*

Indians that had been given to me." This was a common feeling among many European officers during the war. Labeled as savages, the Native Americans were thought to be more concerned with murder and plunder than actually waging war. Along with the Caughnawagas, members of the Abenakis, Algonquins and Nipissings made up the remainder of the French allied Indian force.[54]

When on campaign, native warriors were usually accompanied or even led by an officer of the Troupes de la Marine. During the campaign of 1755, overall command of Dieskau's warriors was given to fifty-three-year-old Jacques Legardeur de St. Pierre, a native of Montreal and career soldier in the colonial forces. "An officer of superior merit," according to Vaudreuil, St. Pierre had spent most of the first half of the decade in various outposts throughout the Ohio River Valley. In 1753, he commanded the garrison at Fort LeBeouf when young George Washington visited with direct orders from Governor Dinwiddie for the French to evacuate the area that rightfully belonged to King George II. Washington noted that St. Pierre was "an elderly gentleman with much the air of a soldier." The response that Washington received from his French counterpart was not quite what he was yearning for. St. Pierre, the devoted and intelligent officer that he was, refused to act on an order from a royal governor who had no authority over him or his subordinates. This sent Washington packing back to Williamsburg to report to Dinwiddie. Two years later, he returned north to Montreal and was given command of the native contingent fighting with Dieskau's army. St. Pierre was respected by the warriors and by his fellow Canadians. His experience and leadership through the wilderness of North America was to be crucial to France's military success as the army departed from Canada and moved on Lake Ontario that summer. The French campaign was now fully commencing, and so, too, was England's.[55]

4

THE CAMPAIGNS OF 1755

BRADDOCK'S MARCH AND THE BATTLE OF THE MONONGAHELA

The centerpiece of England's four-pronged thrust against the French in North America in the summer of 1755 was Major General Edward Braddock's campaign to capture Fort Duquesne at the Forks of the Ohio River. The movement, according to Braddock's instructions from the Duke of Cumberland, was of "the greatest importance, and therefore demands the utmost care." It was critical to suppress the French threat in western Pennsylvania if Great Britain was to rightfully secure its possessions in North America. To accomplish this task, Braddock was given the Forty-fourth and Forty-eighth Regiments of Foot, then serving in Ireland and both extremely understrength. To increase the sizes of these two units, the general hoped to fill their ranks with colonial levies and volunteers upon arriving in America. As commander in chief he held authority not only over all regular regiments in the colonies and Nova Scotia but also over the provincial regiments and militias. This extreme power over the colonists was not well received, and Braddock's stern and robotic personality quickly fell out of favor; he was seen more as a military dictator than the man who would liberate the colonists from their immediate threats to the north and west.[56]

Braddock set sail for America with his military family (staff) on December 22, 1754, ahead of the Forty-fourth and Forty-eighth Regiments. He hoped to arrive early in America and begin organizing his means of supplying his army and also to meet with the royal governors of the colonies, who would be offering the most aid during the upcoming campaign season. The winter voyage was harsh and trying for the men onboard the *Norwich* and *Centurion*, but the general understood it was a necessary risk to take; the frozen waters of the St. Lawrence River would not allow the French to send reinforcements to Quebec until the ice thawed in the spring. His party arrived in Hampton Roads, Virginia, on February 19, 1755. He then moved to the Virginia colonial capital, Williamsburg, arriving four days later to meet with Governor Dinwiddie. The two discussed various topics, including the development of events in the Ohio River Valley and what the colony would supply for the expedition. While in Williamsburg during this time, the Forty-fourth and Forty-eighth Regiments of Foot arrived in Virginia and quartered themselves in Alexandria, much to the dismay of the small Potomac River town's inhabitants.

After his stay in Williamsburg and a long month of issuing a plethora of logistical orders for his army, Braddock and Dinwiddie traveled to Annapolis, Maryland, and conferred with Royal Governor Horatio Sharpe before making their way to Alexandria, where the governors of Massachusetts, New York and Pennsylvania were set to meet them. In the middle of April the Carlyle House Congress was held, and all plans were laid out before the colonial governors. Their lack of excitement to open their purses and fund the expedition surprised Braddock, to say the least. Following the conference, Braddock wrote to the Duke of Newcastle: "As very little assistance has already been offered me by the provinces and still less is to be expected from them, it is necessary for me to apprise your grace that my contingent account will be much greater than I had persuaded myself, or than, I believe, Your Grace imagines." The general's contempt for the colonists began to grow. It seemed as if he was undertaking something much greater than he imagined. Regardless, his duty was to king and country, and he was determined to see that his mission yielded no other results than ultimate victory over the French.[57]

The first trek of Braddock's March would be to Fort Cumberland. Two routes were taken by his army to its destination. In the middle of April, Sir Peter Halkett's Forty-fourth Regiment of Foot advanced to Winchester, Virginia, with the artillery and supply train, while Colonel Thomas Dunbar's Forty-eighth Regiment traveled to Frederick, Maryland. Braddock moved his camp with the Forty-eighth Regiment and met with Pennsylvanian Benjamin Franklin to discuss the possibility of procuring more wagons for the expedition, which Franklin succeeded in doing. On April 29, Dunbar's regiment departed from Frederick and moved west toward the Potomac

River crossing at Conococheague (Williamsport, Maryland), beginning a 129-mile march to Fort Cumberland. Braddock accompanied the Forty-eighth over South Mountain before turning south, crossing the Potomac with his military family at present-day Shepherdstown, West Virginia, and making his way to Winchester to rendezvous with the bulk of his army. Now riding beside the general as a volunteer aide-de-camp was George Washington, who had refused to accept a commission as a captain in the Virginia independent companies. After arriving in Winchester, Braddock moved to catch up with the divided segments of Halkett's force, which had been moving toward Wills Creek at a much quicker pace than Dunbar's column. They were following a ninety-seven-mile-long road constructed by Deputy Quartermaster General Sir John St. Clair. On May 10, Braddock and his army began arriving at Fort Cumberland.[58]

The expeditionary force assembling along Wills Creek at Fort Cumberland was composed of approximately twenty-four hundred men. The army was divided into a First and Second Brigade with Halkett and Dunbar, respectively, in command. Along with the seven hundred men of the Forty-fourth Regiment of Foot were four independent companies from Maryland and Virginia and one from New York commanded by the future "victor" of the Battle of Saratoga, Horatio Gates. Dunbar's brigade was composed of his own Forty-eighth Regiment of Foot and also six provincial companies from North Carolina, South Carolina and Virginia. Braddock's artillery train was small for the size of his force, but it still flaunted twenty-seven pieces of various sizes. The one thing that the expeditionary force lacked, however, was crucial to the success of the force moving through the vast North American wilderness: Native American allies.[59]

Historians have debated for centuries Edward Braddock and his use of—or lack of use of—the Ohio River Valley Indians. Stories and some primary accounts have been passed down that claim the general had extremely offended the Indians who met with him at Fort Cumberland in the spring of 1755, when he supposedly proclaimed that "No savage should inherit the land" after the British beat the French off of it. The natives believed that if they could not regain what had always been their own, then they would lend their assistance to someone else; in this case, the French. On May 29, when Braddock's army departed Fort Cumberland to begin its final trek of about 110 miles to Fort Duquesne, only eight warriors stuck around.[60]

For the final leg of the journey to the Forks of the Ohio River, fourteen hundred men were sent forward as part of a "flying column," while the remainder of the force and the heavy artillery remained behind with Thomas Dunbar. The two wings of the army did not march in synchronization, and on the morning of July 9, when the first column forded the Monongahela River and approached Fort Duquesne, Dunbar's portion of the army was nearly sixty miles behind. With fife and drum beating "The Grenadier's March" as Braddock and the forward column splashed across the river in full sight of the French, Lieutenant Colonel Thomas Gage was sent ahead with a hand-picked body of men to assess the situation. Only several miles from the fort, Gage was attacked by nine hundred Canadian marines, militia and French-allied Indians (Ottawas, Shawnees, Delawares and Mingos) sent by the commandant of Duquesne and led by Captain Daniel Beaujeu. Almost immediately, Beaujeu was struck and killed by a stray bullet and organization began to crumble within the Canadian ranks, but the native warriors took cover behind rocks and trees paralleling Braddock's road. The forward British column crumbled under the immense pressure by an enemy hidden among the forest and retreated down the woodland trail, colliding with the second half of the column moving toward the sound of the guns. Confusion grew as Braddock urged his men to fight in a linear style in the road, instead of adapting to their environment and combating the Canadians and Indians in a similar manner. Casualties mounted, and Braddock was severely wounded while bravely trying to maintain order. The whole army fled the field and rushed to meet up with Dunbar's column, which was well beyond supporting distance. After several hours of bloody combat the Battle of the Monongahela was over, and nearly nine hundred British and provincial soldiers had fallen. It truly was one of the greatest defeats ever dealt to the British army in its long and esteemed history.[61]

On the road back to Fort Cumberland, Major General Edward Braddock succumbed to his wounds and died on July 13. A funeral was held the following day as he was laid to rest in the middle of the road. His young protégé, George Washington—who had amazingly escaped the battle unscathed—read a short sermon. With the death of Braddock and also Sir Peter Halkett, command of the retreating force belonged to Dunbar. Incredibly, rather than reorganizing his force and moving again to attack the French, he ordered his army to advance to Philadelphia and go into winter quarters—in the middle of the summer! This decision left the Maryland, Pennsylvania and Virginia frontiers wide open to French and Indian raiding parties, which they took full advantage of, wreaking havoc on the English settlers. It was a dark time in the history of the American colonies. The killing and pillaging continued until 1758, when another British expeditionary

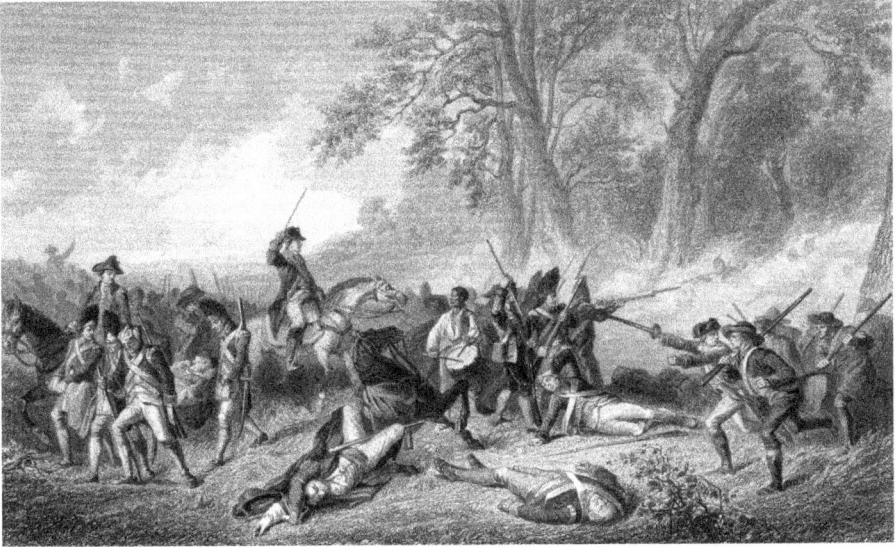

The Battle of the Monongahela. *Courtesy of New York Public Library Digital Collections.*

force, this time commanded by John Forbes, finally ousted the French from the Ohio River Valley and sent them fleeing north.

Braddock's defeat along the banks of the Monongahela was a crushing blow for England in the summer of 1755. The failure of Braddock's army to capture Fort Duquesne and subsequently join forces with Shirley to assault Fort Niagara meant that the Massachusetts politician-turned-soldier would be on his own with what men and supplies he had at his immediate disposal. Not only did this great task suddenly fall into his lap, but with the death of General Braddock, William Shirley also became commander in chief in North America. The fate of the remaining campaigns became his responsibility. Luckily for him, in Nova Scotia, Robert Monckton had already accomplished his mission.

MONCKTON'S CAMPAIGN IN NOVA SCOTIA

With the terrible news of the British defeat in Pennsylvania came a glimmer of hope for the success of the 1755 campaigns. In Nova Scotia, particularly Acadia, the smallest of the four British expeditionary forces had completed its mission of subduing the French garrisons at Forts

Beauséjour and Gaspereau along the Chignecto Isthmus. These twin victories secured the French-influenced populations and subsequently led to the first ethnic cleansing in modern history: *Le Grand Dérangement*, or the Expulsion of the Acadians.

Following the Treaty of Utrecht in 1713 that ended the War of Spanish Succession, the French colony of Acadia (Nova Scotia, New Brunswick and Prince Edward Island) was ceded to England, and its inhabitants were forced to take an oath of loyalty to the Crown; many refused to do so. For the next forty years the Acadian people were steadfast in their resolve to maintain their French-influenced culture and Catholic religion and quickly became a thorn in the side of the British Empire. Militia units were constantly active and serving beside France's colonial and regular soldiers fighting in the province against England during the proceeding conflicts. Using Fort Beauséjour and Louisbourg—which was returned to France as part of the Treaty of Aix-la-Chappelle following its 1745 capture—as major military supply bases, the possibility of a large-scale Acadian uprising remained a great threat. Thus, in 1754, as the plans for the following year's campaigns began to formulate in London, suppressing Nova Scotia and ridding it of all French influence became a priority.[62]

Working closely with Nova Scotia's royal governor Charles Lawrence, Braddock and William Shirley gave command of a small, twenty-two-hundred-man force to capture Forts Beauséjour and Gaspereau to Lieutenant Colonel Robert Monckton and Major John Winslow. Monckton, who commanded a detachment of 270 regulars and also outranked Winslow, was in charge of the expedition. About 2,000 provincials from the Boston area were recruited and placed under Winslow's command and departed from the Bay Colony on May 26, destined for Annapolis Royal in the Bay of Fundy. There, they rendezvoused with the regulars and the artillery. On June 1, the force sailed for the Chignecto Isthmus and garrisoned at Fort Lawrence along the Missaguash River—the staging area for the campaign.[63]

In the weeks that followed, Monckton's force advanced west to Fort Beauséjour, fighting minor skirmishes with small French and Indian parties, suffering minimal casualties and securing the necessary avenue of approach. A vivid account of the siege and subsequent surrender was left behind by John Brewse, an engineer serving under Monckton. He recalled in October to the Board of Trade:

> *The troops continued their March to a riseing Ground, within a mile and a half of the French Fort, when the Enemy set Fire to the Village and*

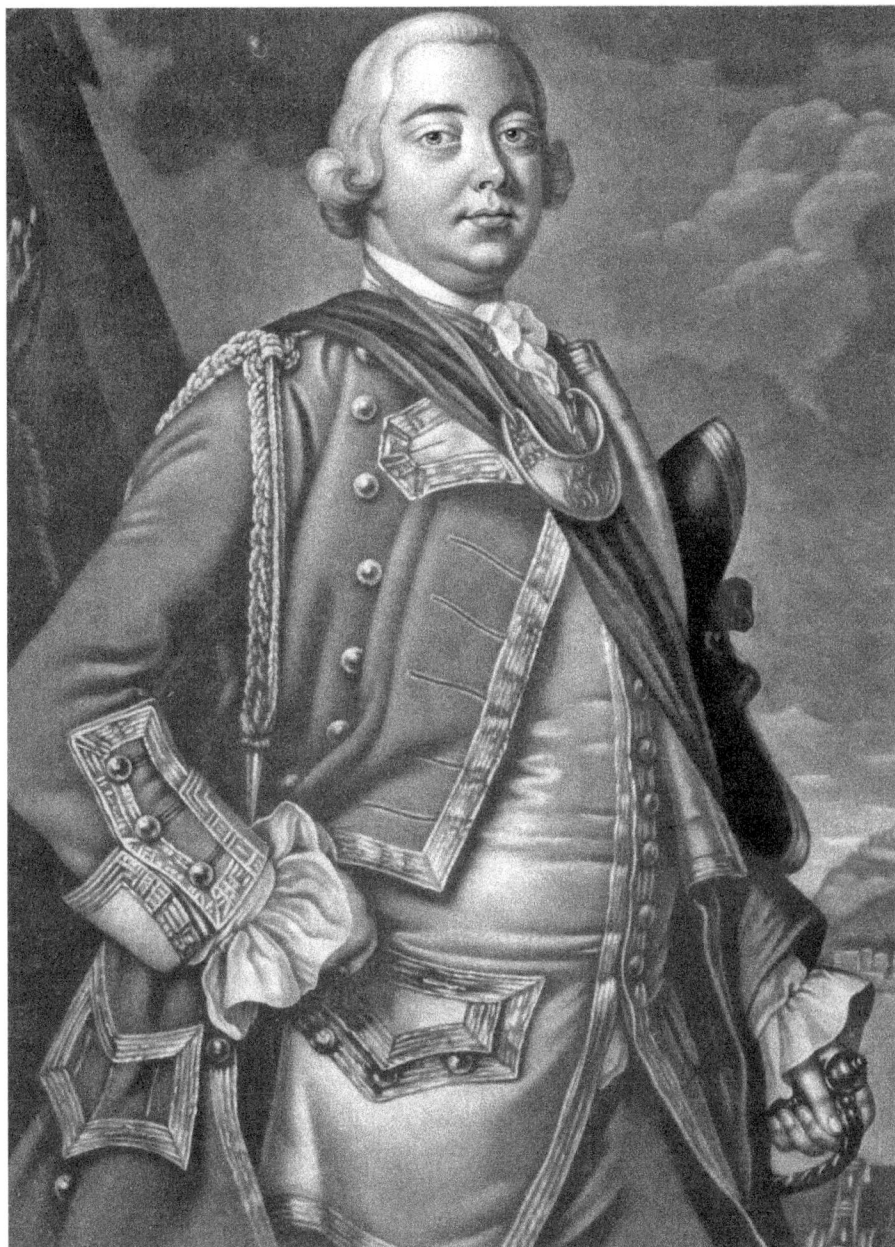

Colonel Robert Monckton. *Courtesy of New York Public Library Digital Collections.*

Church. The next day we cleared the Woods for an Encampment from the riseing Ground beforementioned in a Line to the Marsh, thro' which the River [Missaguash] *runs, and where the Vessels were to lye that contained Stores and Provisions. From this time to the 12ᵗʰ we continued reconnoitering and landing our Cannon, and on the evening of that day we dislodged a Body of French and Indians from the Ground on which the approaches were to be made. In this Affair Ensign Tongue was wounded; He was one of three Officers appointed to assist me as Engineers. We remained in possession of the Ground, but the intrenching Tools not coming up 'till midnight it was impossible to undertake the work I had proposed, as we had but three hours till daylight, so that I traced a parallel of two hundred yards and lodged the Men in security, which was all we were able to effect, for the next morning the Garrison kept an incessant Fire from six pieces of Cannon. However on the 14ᵗʰ we a Boyau or Trench of Approach to the Right, and the next night another to the Left. A thirteen Inch Mortar, and three of eight inches were placed on our left beyond the parallel, which had the desired effect, for by ten in the morning on the 16ᵗʰ the Commandant* [Louis Du Pont Duchambon de Vergor] *sent out to Capitulate, Articles were exchanged before dark.*[64]

The five hundred besieged French soldiers and Acadian militiamen inside the fort never stood a chance against Monckton's overwhelming numbers. "On the morning of the 16ᵗʰ," according to one French soldier garrisoned in Beauséjour, "an enemy bomb exploded on one of the casements to the left of the entrance. . . . It was enough to bring about the surrender of the fort because fire combined with inexperience made everyone in that place give up." The following day, the commanding officer at Fort Gaspereau, knowing that his situation was hopeless and that his men would only suffer the same fate as Vergor's, asked to take part in the capitulation discussions. The combined regular-provincial force had taken Gaspereau without it even firing a single shot in anger. Monckton's victory on the Chignecto Isthmus left the French with only Louisbourg in Nova Scotia and spelled doom for the Acadian populace.[65]

In October 1755, the expulsion began under strict orders of Charles Lawrence. All Acadians, even those who had not taken part in any form of social upheaval, were rounded up by military force and shipped to the colonies and Europe. During the next nine years, upward of 11,500 Acadians were deported or fled their homes and replaced by Anglo American farmers who recolonized the province. A measure taken in response to a threat to national security, the *Grand Dérangement* was an extremely dark and tragic period in the history of the western world. Following the Seven Years' War in 1764, the British government passed an order-in-council to allow the Acadian people to return to the place they once called home.[66]

As the French forts on the Chignecto Isthmus fell in concert to Monckton and Winslow in the middle of June 1755, in Albany the men who would take part in Johnson and Shirley's campaigns against Crown Point and Niagara began to organize and prepare for the coming summer.

Shirley's Campaign against Fort Niagara

The feud that developed between Johnson and Shirley in the summer of 1755 doomed the Fort Niagara campaign from the very beginning. The fight to obtain supplies and native allies for the expedition did nothing but slow progress and hamper any prospect of success as Shirley's men left Albany to make the 250-mile trek to Oswego. Shirley's employment of the crooked John Henry Lydius broke relations with Johnson and left him without Iroquois support. It was Johnson's duty to recruit warriors for the expeditions, not Lydius's, and the attempt by Shirley to go over the New Yorker's head only intensified the bitter rivalry that would lead to his downfall the following year. During that summer, Shirley would have to go to Oswego alone with only the troops he had at his disposal. In Johnson's opinion, it was not necessary for the Fort Niagara expedition to be accompanied by any native warriors when it would be moving strictly through friendly territory. Johnson took the Mohawks; in response, Shirley took the Jersey Blues.

One of the largest disadvantages for the men being sent to Oswego was the route from Albany to the fort. It was a 250-mile journey over land and water that would be even more difficult if weather conditions were not right. All in all, the march to Oswego took roughly three weeks. It began at Albany and followed the Mohawk River for forty-five miles to the Oneida Carry, where an overland portage was taken to Wood Creek. The tributary eventually entered the Oswego River, which in turn was used to carry the men to Fort Oswego. If any of these waterways were frozen or too rough to be traversed by boat, travel became hampered and resulted in severe logistical headaches. Albany was the main supply base for the northern campaigns in 1755, making an overextended supply line another problem for William Shirley.[67]

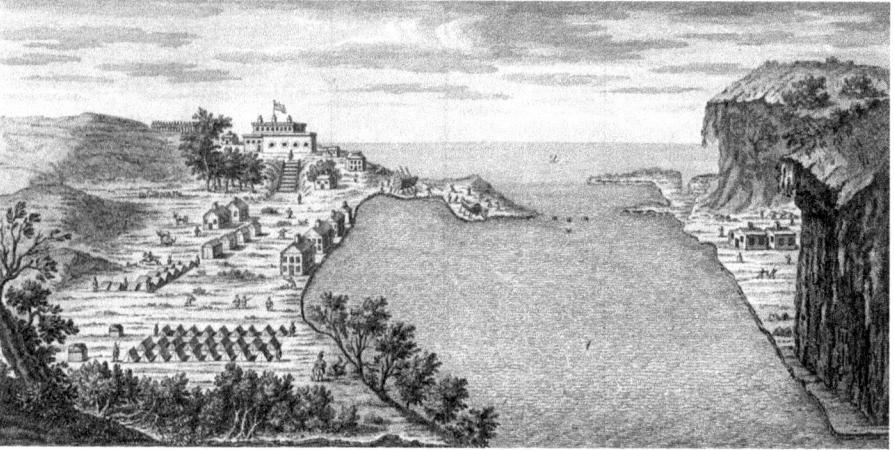

A south view of Fort Oswego on Lake Ontario, William Shirley's base of operations. *Courtesy of New York Public Library Digital Collections.*

Fort Niagara, constructed in 1726 by the French in order to neutralize English trade in the Great Lakes region, was the main supply artery for the Ohio River Valley. Capturing Fort Niagara would spell disaster for the French at Fort Duquesne and the other outposts south of Lake Ontario. Even with Braddock's expedition failing, Fort Duquesne could still be forced into submission if Shirley could succeed in capturing Niagara. It was an opportunity to redeem the late Braddock and the English cause in North America, but as Shirley would find out that summer, it was a lot easier said than done.

On August 17, Shirley and the sixteen hundred or so men from the First New Jersey Regiment, Fiftieth and Fifty-first Regiments of Foot, as well as one hundred or so natives who were recruited along the way, arrived at Fort Oswego. To the commanding general's dismay, it was discovered that the fortification was in shambles. Garrisoned by only an independent company of New Yorkers, not much work had been done to maintain the fort or its outer works. It was clear that if the British desired for Oswego to be its major military outpost and staging area along Lake Ontario, repairs and renovations needed to be made.

France's presence in the Great Lakes region was large enough to present a serious threat to Shirley's campaign. Not only was Fort Niagara garrisoned sufficiently, but roughly fifty miles to the north of Oswego another fort—Frontenac—housed a force of Canadians and Indians equal in strength to Shirley's. The enemy garrison at Fort Frontenac actually imposed a greater threat to the English than Niagara's. When Braddock's army retreated from the Monongahela battlefield that summer it left behind among the dead and wounded a complete set of plans for the English North American campaigns that year. Because of this, the French along Lake Ontario knew very well that Shirley was at Oswego and what his objectives were. If Shirley's army moved west to besiege Niagara, the garrison at Frontenac could move south, take Oswego, trap the British force and cut it off from the eastern colonies and any hope of rescue. The commander in chief was well aware of this dangerous prospect and, at a council of war later that month, determined that it was more important to strengthen Oswego against this threat and hold off on capturing Niagara until the following year, when the army could be better supplied.[68]

The campaign against the French at Fort Niagara was over before it really truly began. The following month, William Shirley left Fort Oswego and returned to Albany before making his way to New York City to tend to his new duties as commander in chief. Seven hundred men were left behind to strengthen the fortification's defenses. Unfortunately for these poor souls, they were doomed to suffer from a lack of supplies and provisions in the upcoming winter and were left to be captured by a French army under the Marquis de Montcalm the following year.

These were the campaigns of 1755 taking place throughout North America in a year of undeclared open warfare. The Crown Point expedition—the final piece of England's four-pronged offensive—was taking shape in the spring and summer as the other armies moved toward victory and defeat. In the wake of Braddock's defeat along the Monongahela and Shirley's abandonment of the Niagara campaign, the stakes were as high as they could possibly be with Johnson and his provincials. It became a time when only a victory could matter.

5

THE CROWN POINT EXPEDITION

*J*une 1755 brought an incredible amount of hustle and bustle to the small city of Albany as troops filed in from New England, New Jersey and New York to organize for the expeditions against Crown Point and Fort Niagara. In the final week of June, companies from Connecticut's two regiments arrived and encamped south of the city. They were followed by the First Rhode Island provincials; Cockcroft and Fitch's New Yorkers and Connecticut men; the First, Second and Third Massachusetts; the Jersey Blues; and the remainder of the First and Second Connecticut. Blanchard's First New Hampshire was weeks away from arriving. On June 30, Phineas Lyman, in William Johnson's absence, assumed command of the Crown Point expeditionary force. With all of its military inhabitants, Albany became one of the most populated cities in the English colonies.[69]

Albany is one of the oldest remaining cities in America from the colonial era. Originally, the area served as a crucial post for Dutch and Native American fur traders, and Fort Orange was constructed there in 1624. By the 1670s, however, England had taken possession of New York, and the settlement was renamed after the Duke of Albany. According to nineteenth-century historian Francis Parkman, when the soldiers came to Albany in the summer of 1755, the city consisted of:

> the great street, grassy and broad, that descended thence to the river, with market, guard-house, town-hall, and two churches in the middle, and rows of quaint Dutch-built houses on both sides, each detached from its neighbors,

each with its well, garden, and green, and its great overshadowing tree.
Before every house was a capacious porch, with seats where the people
gathered in the summer twilight; old men at one door, matrons at another,
young men and girls mingling at a third; while the cows with their tinkling
bells came from the common at the end of the town, each stopping to be
milked at the door of its owner; and children, porringer in hand, sat on the
steps, watching the process and waiting their evening meal.[70]

The gay and peaceful scene was certain to change as rows of soldiers' tents
littered the city and its outskirts and the martial sounds of drilling echoed in
the air. Thousands of men from the Northern Colonies gathered to begin a
great and terrible adventure.

The duty of placing each regiment in its own designated place of
encampment fell on the shoulders of newly arrived British regular officer
Captain William Eyre. An active member of the Forty-fourth Regiment
of Foot, Eyre was sent to New York by General Braddock and given the
unenviable workload of serving as Johnson's chief engineer, chief of
artillery and quartermaster general—all vacant positions that needed to
be filled. "He seems to be an active capable officer," William Johnson
wrote to Shirley from his home at Mount Johnson on June 16. "He tells
me he thinks he can execute that Duty & is willing to do so. Such an
officer is absolutely necessary." Eyre
also held the distinction of being the
only regular soldier serving with the
Crown Point army. It was fortunate
for Eyre that he was dispatched to
New York, for he was able to miss
being part of the disaster along the
Monongahela, where he certainly
could have lost his life like the majority
of Braddock's officers in the field that
day. In Albany, the captain kept busy
for the first few weeks after his arrival,
establishing encampment sites north
and south of the city and employing
carpenters and blacksmiths to build
carriages for the artillery, including
four- and six-pound brass guns, and
to repair already damaged pieces.[71]

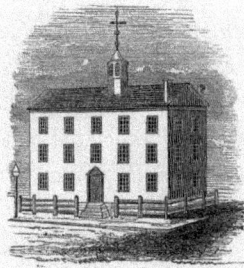

Albany Courthouse, 1754. *Courtesy of New
York Public Library Digital Collections.*

While Eyre was hard at work making sure the army was in a sufficient enough condition to move against the French, William Johnson made his way to Albany on July 7 from his vigorous meetings with the Iroquois at his home along the Mohawk River. That evening, Lieutenant Colonel Seth Pomeroy of the Third Massachusetts Regiment, along with a handful of other provincial officers, had supper with the general and got their first taste of who the man was. "So far as I am acquainted with Mr. Johnson," Pomeroy wrote to his wife, Mary, back in Northampton, "he appears like a Gentleman: & with a grate deal of modesty yet free & Pleasent." Three days later William Shirley arrived as well and "at his arrival the Cannon in the Fort ware Discharg'd [and] the Field officers that ware in Town waited upon the Governor & Drank [a] glass of wine with him." The martial pomp and circumstance was alive in Albany as reviews were held and the officers continued to dine and drink like royalty and toast to their confidence in a quick and easy victory over the French that summer. "I had the agreeable news by Governor Shirley at Diner yesterday of Adm[i]ral Boscawen['s] Further success upon [the] French Fleet," Pomeroy recorded in his journal on July 16. "I Can't But hope [this] is [the] Beginning of a mighty work that God in his Providence is about to do for us this year."[72]

The army's time spent in Albany was short-lived. On July 17, William Johnson issued the first orders for a movement north. General Lyman was given the task of moving to the Great Carrying Place along the Hudson River, where he was to "erect Log Magazines covered with Bark Sufficient to contain & secure from the Weather, the Ammunition[,] Provisions [and so on] belonging to the Army." Along the way, Lyman's men were ordered to:

> open the Road Twenty five to thirty feet wide where it will possibly admit of it, to have the Trees, Logs & all obstructions cleared away, the Stumps trim[m]ed close, Bridges well repaired where necessary & good Ones made where wanted, on the whole as good a Road made for Carriage as possible, and besides the officers who are over the workmen you will please to take a review your self. As you are well apprized of the Sudden & lurking attacks of the Enemy, I make no doubt but you will so dispose your Troops & keep up such a Discipline amongst them, as will secure the whole Body from any reproachful Insults from the Scouting parties of the Enemy.[73]

To accomplish constructing the storehouses and renovating the road from Albany to the Great Carrying Place, Lyman was given the First Connecticut, Ruggles's First Massachusetts and Williams's Third Massachusetts

Regiment, as well as two brass field pieces. Well aware that the men serving in the ranks of these units were green and had "not been used to a Regular Military Life," Johnson recommended to Lyman that he "keep up as strict a Discipline as Circumstances will possibly admit of...to establish and preserve that due Obedience...without which every kind of Military Undertaking will be Shameful & probably fatal." All preparations were made for the first leg of the campaign, and by July 22, Lyman and his men were on the move north.[74]

The first day's march for the contingent went rather well. According to Captain Elisha Hawley of the Third Massachusetts, the three regiments made their way roughly twelve miles above the city before setting up along the Hudson River and lightening the loads on the bateaux that were to carry them up the waterway. By the twenty-fourth, the men had arrived at Stillwater and pitched their tents on the east side of the river. That night the officers, including Seth Pomeroy—who had earlier "Set out with a guard of 100 men to guard ye waggons"—dined together with General Lyman. This would be the first of five nights spent by the advance party at Stillwater.[75]

For the next four days Lyman's men were encamped at Stillwater, where men were sent out in numerous working parties and "employ'ed in Clearing the road [from Albany] for ye Waggons to Come with our Stores," according to Captain Hawley. Military logistics can be a nightmare for an army on the move, especially when venturing through thick wilderness and across rivers by boat. It is one thing to move an army of thousands of men and cannons, but those same soldiers must remain supplied with ammunition, food and tools. As chief quartermaster of Johnson's army, Captain Eyre would have had the bulk of this work thrown on his shoulders when he came north to Albany. It was to the Crown Point army's benefit to have a professionally trained regular officer managing these affairs. Not only could an army's infrastructure hamper a campaign, but wagon trains and a separated army also were always under the threat of an enemy attack.[76]

Not even a week had passed since Lyman's wing of the army had left Albany, and already the fear of being attacked began to make the general uneasy. "You are quite right to be in constant preparation against any Attack from the Enemy," William Johnson wrote Lyman on the twenty-seventh in response to the possibility of an early fight. "Tho it may not happen it will en[s]ure the Soldiers to that cautious readiness [that] is most essential to our preservation & Success." Although the French were not known to be anywhere south of Crown Point, the possibility of hostile Indians lurking in the woods hugging the road to the Great Carrying Place caused the New Englanders to remain on alert. At any moment the enemy could attack and impede the progress of the campaign and maybe even end the hope of a victory in New York that summer.[77]

The prospect of having the advance to Lake Champlain come to an early end prompted William Shirley to prepare a contingency plan. While Lyman's men trudged north, the provisional commander in chief scribbled off new orders for William Johnson from Schenectady:

> *Sir,*
>
> *I think it necessary for His Majesty's Service to Send you the following Instructions. . . .*
>
> *In Case you should meet with Such Difficulties in the Expedition now under your Command against the Incroachments of the French at Crown Point, and upon Lake Champlain, from a Superior Force of the Enemy, as shall oblige you to quit the Attempt, You are to make your Retreat with the Army to the City of Albany, there to remain with it, for the Defence and Protection of that place; as also to cover the whole Province of New York against any Attack of the French and Indians from Canada, until you shall receive further Orders: You are also to take all Opportunities of acquainting me at Oswego or elsewhere with your Proceedings in the aforesaid Expedition.[78]*

As the campaigns commenced that summer in western and Upstate New York, it became clear to Johnson that his primary mission was the reduction of the French fort at Crown Point. Should that fail, his duty was to defend Albany and the rest of the colony from any further enemy advance. Should Albany fall to the French, Shirley's force at Oswego would be cut off from all support and supplies, and Upstate New York and New England would have their communication lines severed from the rest of the English colonies. Timing was everything, and Johnson's army needed to move fast before the French could seize the initiative and attack.

By July 29 Lyman's force was on the move again. Orders were given to march to Saratoga; before noon all of the "Stores ware put into ye Battoes," according to Seth Pomeroy, "& we all March'd off...with our 2 Field Brass Peases[,] and a number of men to guard on Each Side [of] ye river." They arrived at their destination around five o'clock that evening. For the next two days more working parties of roughly three hundred men were sent north to clear and widen the road. Captain John Burk of the Third Massachusetts was sent forward with "30 men to see what I could discover, but saw nothing." That same day, 1,114 cannonballs were unearthed at the site of an old fort that had been burned during King George's War to prevent it from falling into the hands of the French. The following afternoon, Lyman's wing moved four miles farther with its 180 bateaux, which had to be dragged up small falls that fell roughly six or seven feet into the river. "It was fatiguing," according to Burk. "This day the men had half a pint of rum more than the allowance." The expedition so far had been a success, and Lyman's regiments were only two days away from reaching the Great Carrying Place. However, back in Albany, news had arrived of Braddock's disaster along the Monongahela.[79]

The defeat of the British regular and provincial army in western Pennsylvania left little room for failure along the Hudson River–Lake George–Lake Champlain corridor. As early as July 27, reports began to filter into Albany regarding the French victory. "There are Reports about General Braddock's Troops & Not favorable Ones," Johnson wrote in his letter to Lyman dated that same day, "but I [received] yesterday Letter from New York, [which] tell me they look upon these Reports as False, Treacherous & Groundless." Unfortunately for Johnson, those claims from New York were actually the false ones. On August 1, the commanding general penned a letter to Braddock's wounded aide-de-camp, Robert Orme:

> Dear Sir,
>
> How deeply I am affected by our Loss on the Ohio & by poor General Braddock's Death I will not attempt to describe nor expatiate on the Tragical Subject. To me in particular & I dare say to all who know you Your escape with Life is an essential Consolation under so Melancholly an Event. I do most unfeignedly felicitate you thereupon & hope your wounds will be soon healed, your Health reestablished & your future Life yield you every desirable Good....
>
> Since the unfortunate Turn of Affairs, I am under great Fears that our Indians will not dare to appear in our favour, and I am sensible it will increase the utility of Mr. Shirley's having more Indians with him at Oswego. And without Indians it would be madness to undertake the Expedition to Crown Point.
>
> I have had a few Indians with me since the bad News [which] I imparted to them & they told me it should not alter their resolutions. I am waiting to see what effect it will have on the several Nations of Indians, and till that point is cleared up I must let all things remain as they are.[80]

The Battle of the Monongahela was a crushing blow to the prospect of British military success in North America that year and, as Johnson feared, was something that could strain the various Indian alliances with his and Shirley's armies. France clearly held the upper hand, and its victory in the Ohio River Valley could have easily pushed the neutral tribes to its aid. Luckily for Johnson, King Hendrick and his Mohawk warriors did "not alter their resolutions."

The same day that the letter was written to Robert Orme, a new set of orders was dispatched to Colonel Moses Titcomb of the Second Massachusetts Regiment. With Lyman's wing of the army, or first division, making progress in its advance to the Great Carrying Place, and with the military road now wide enough to support a speedy march, Johnson ordered Titcomb to take command of the second division and prepare it to depart. With Titcomb would march his own regiment, Second Connecticut, and the remaining companies of the Third Massachusetts Regiment. Also included in the column would be the bulk of the artillery train of "Two 32 pounders, Two 18 pounders, Two 12 pounders [and] Four Iron 6 pounders," supply wagons and the necessary bateaux needed to carry the force. Before setting off, Titcomb conducted a thorough inspection of the men's arms, ammunition and accoutrements and read them the Articles of War against mutiny and desertion. Writing later that day to his wife from his regiment's camp north of the city, Lieutenant Colonel Nathan Whiting of the Second Connecticut relayed a powerful message of his devotion and faith that would carry him through the upcoming campaign:

> *My dearest wife,*
>
> *I am here much Longer than I expected When I left you[.] Tis unhappy on many Accounts that we have delayed so long, but know not that it could be prevented. [W]e have orders now to March and . . . tis probable I shall not have opportunity to write you again till I get to the Carrying Place I doubt your tender concern for me my dear will fill you with too many uneasy apprehensions & fears for my Safety Which I fear will be much increased upon hearing of the unhappy disaster of General Braddock but Let Not that trouble you my dear[.] God is my Safeguard and defense & I Trust has better things in store for his people than to give them all a prey Into the hands of their enemys—we are never more discouraged on Account of that defeat but Rather Animated with the greater Resolution to go on, we may have more enemys to encounter so that we may want more Strength, or our conquests will be more Glorious or our defeat less Shameful but the Latter I hope & believe Will Not be the Case. Pray make your Self as easy as possible I know your Dayly prayers*

are for my preservation Let it be an article of them that it not be obtained
by any unworthy means, but in the prosecution of the Duty I owe at this
time to my Self, my Country & my God.[81]

By August 6, Whiting and the rest of Titcomb's column were advancing to the Great Carrying Place to rendezvous with the first division.[82]

Three days prior to Titcomb's division's departure from Albany, Lyman's wing of the army arrived at the Great Carrying Place along the bend in the Hudson River around six o'clock at night, about fifty miles north of Albany. The area was the former site of Fort Nicholson as well as John Henry Lydius's Indian trading post. Now it would be the home of Fort Lyman. Immediately upon arrival men began gathering material for the storehouses and fortified encampment even through the heavy rain that came that night. This task occupied the Connecticut and Massachusetts men for the next several days. During that time a court-martial was held by Lyman in camp, and on August 6 one soldier "was whip'd 100 stripes for the most vile Cursing & Swareing."[83]

The same day that the punishment was distributed to the convicted soldier, John Burk and nine other men returned to camp from a forward

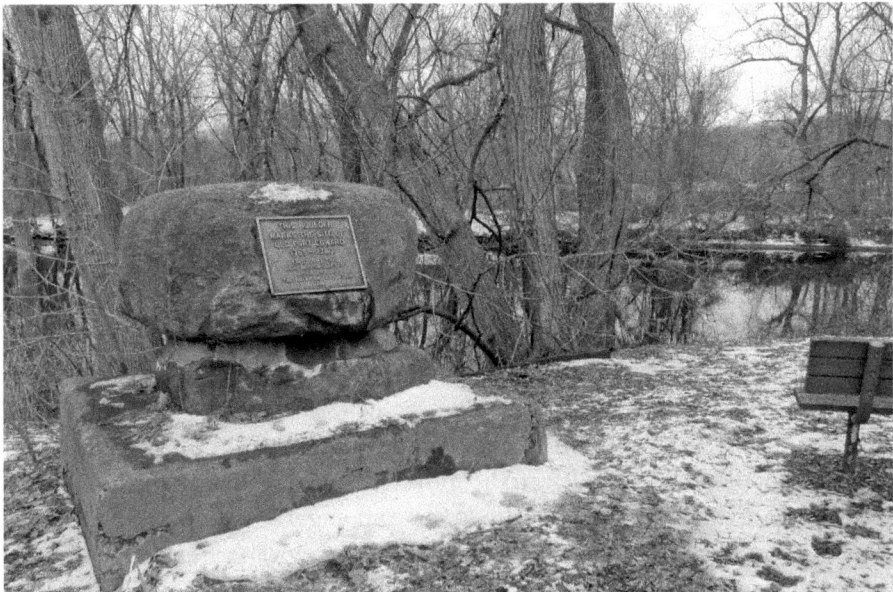

Monument marking the original site of Fort Lyman (Edward), Fort Edward, New York. *Author's collection.*

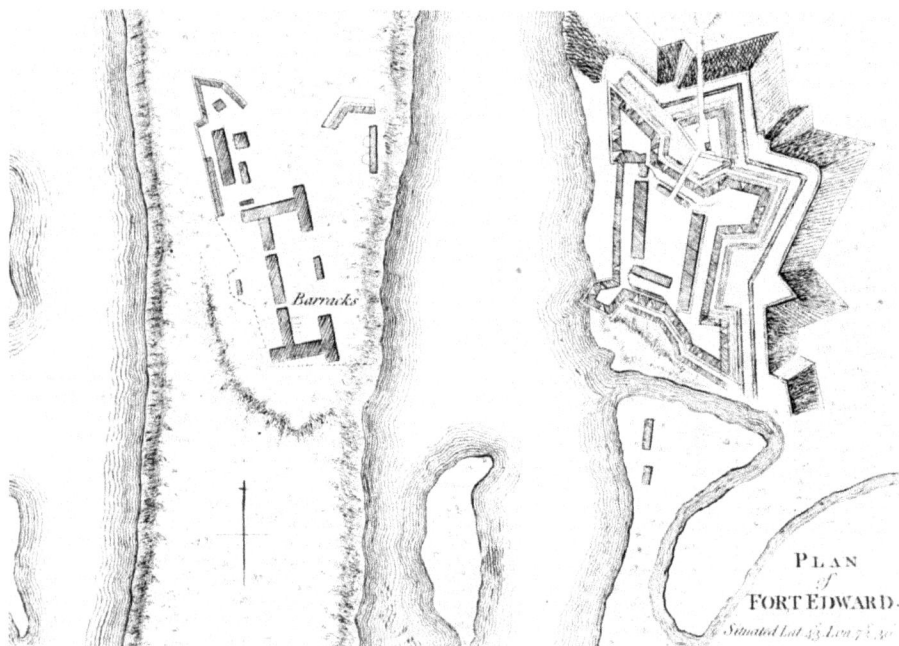

Fort Edward and Roger's Island. *From* A Set of Plans and Forts in North America *(1765)*.

scouting mission to Lake George. There was no sign of any French activity in the area, and all that was accounted for were "3 deer, 1 bear, and an old mare and a wolf." Things were quiet for now, and on August 12 a working party of three hundred men was sent forward to begin clearing and widening the road from the Great Carrying Place to Wood Creek. Two possible routes north existed from the Great Carrying Place. One led to Wood Creek, which could be followed northward directly into Lake Champlain; the other was a direct path of roughly fourteen miles to Lake George. Avoiding the passage of Lake George and instead traveling north via Wood Creek seemed like a more plausible option; Johnson never actually instructed Lyman as to which path would be used by the army. However, it was discovered that the Wood Creek path ran along extremely broken and rough terrain that would make it nearly impossible for artillery to be moved over. Lyman did not wait for the commanding general's opinion, however, and eagerly sent forward his men to clear the Wood Creek road. The rest of the army was on its way up; once both divisions were joined, a general advance was to be made.[84]

Back in Albany, Colonel Joseph Blanchard's First New Hampshire began to arrive on August 11 and 12 and encamped six miles above the city.

68

Johnson himself had departed for the Great Carrying Place the day before and rode ahead of Titcomb's column, and the First New York and First Rhode Island Regiments had begun to march already as well. Blanchard's New Hampshire men had originally been ordered to advance directly to Crown Point across Vermont but were then ordered back and sent to Albany after the exact route to the fort became unclear. Upon his arrival in the city, Blanchard immediately made haste toward the Great Carrying Place, where he hoped to acquaint himself with Johnson and receive orders for his regiment. The colonel rode into Lyman's encampment around nine o'clock in the morning on August 15. Johnson had just arrived the previous day.[85]

The commanding general's entrance into Lyman's camp was met with the welcoming boom of the two field pieces attached to the division. With him came the first element of Mohawk Indians; for many of the New Englanders in the camp, these were the first "savages" they had ever seen in person. James Gilbert of the Third Massachusetts vividly remembered the "od[dness] of Their Dress. They had Juels in Their noses. Their faces painted with all Colouers. They appeared very odious To us also." The presence of the native warriors made the men uneasy. Stories of their supposed barbarous behavior had been passed down from generation to generation and made their way from town to town in New England. Colonel Timothy Ruggles wrote to Johnson on August 16 that a "Proclamation has been made forbidding all persons to sell or give any Rum or strong Liquors to any Indian." This was something that Johnson had stressed to his officers early on in the campaign before the army began moving out of Albany.[86]

As Johnson settled in and established his headquarters on the island in the middle of the Hudson River—later dubbed "Roger's Island" because of its use as the rangers' training site—it was determined by the commanding general that work on the road to Wood Creek should cease immediately. The labor party had completed roughly eight miles when their work was cut short. Scouts were sent out to explore the possibility of any alternate routes, but eventually the road to Lake George was decided on. At the same council of war, Captain Eyre's plan for Fort Lyman was approved, and construction commenced in earnest.

By the time Eyre's proposal for the construction of what would eventually become Fort Lyman was approved, work had already been done by the Connecticut and Massachusetts men encamped along that stretch of the Hudson River. In his journal entry of August 13, Seth Pomeroy described what had been completed thus far:

we finish'd ye Timber work of our Store house which is in ye form on an ["L" shape] 70 foot one way & 40 ye other 15 foot wide at ye North End of it a guard House 30 foot in Length 15 in [width] with a mount upon ye North End of it ye Roof of ye whole Shed Inward upon ye out Side about 12 foot heigh in 2 Stores Port holes to fire out at—a mount at the west Corner upon ye river bank Inclosed from ye West End of ye Store House to ye mount with Stockades & from northwardly End [straight] to ye bank of ye river with ye Same & on ye river bank to ye afore mount at ye west End So Inclosed about half an acre of Land.[87]

By the time the fort was completed the following month, it stood in the shape of a square with three bastions and was surrounded by a ditch and palisade. It could house three hundred men on the inside, and William Eyre believed it was capable of withstanding an attack by an enemy force of fifteen hundred soldiers. The fort was crucial to the defense of the Hudson River as well as the seventy miles of road that now spanned from Albany to Lake George. That new road was an artery—a direct funnel—into the interior of New York. Erecting a fortification at the southern end of the lake to collaborate with Fort Lyman was critical to the defense of the colony.[88]

The next week and some change passed with little to no excitement for the men encamped along the river. Work continued on the fortifications and storehouses, and scouting parties were sent out routinely to search for any sign of the French. On August 17, the First New York Regiment with Cockcroft and Fitch at its head finally arrived, soon followed by Edward Cole's Rhode Islanders. With all but the New Hampshire men now concentrated at Fort Lyman, Johnson's army counted upward of twenty-nine hundred able-bodied men. Two days after the arrival, a council of war was held that determined Johnson and a vanguard of fifteen hundred men would advance to Lake George "as Soon as we Shou[l]d have [Intelligence]" and begin clearing the final stretch of road from the fort. It was also determined at the same meeting that the women accompanying the army should be sent back to Albany.[89]

The behavior of some of the women following the camp had been a grievance of many of the New Englanders. The majority of women traveling with Johnson's army were soldiers' wives or individuals devoting themselves to the cause by traveling with their hometown companies and serving in various roles as cooks, laundresses, nurses and seamstresses. However, there were other camp followers who employed themselves as women of ill-repute. It was this bunch that the New Englanders despised, finding their behavior unchristian and repulsive and a distraction to the men. As early as July 25, Phineas Lyman wrote a letter to Johnson demanding that all women be left behind in Albany:

> *I perceive that there is a number of women coming up with the* [New] *York forces and Rhod*[e] *Island which gives a great uneasiness to ye New England troops and will be if allowd the most Effective stop to the Raising more men in New England than Can be tho't of which I think would be most impolitik at the Time & it would be the Sacrificing all our Character in the Places where we live & some of the officers tell me they believe soldiery will either mob or privately destroy 'em. I think they are of so little Use in the army or Rather none at all that I can't doubt but you will order 'em all to be left behind I had rather Two Soldiers should be dismissed with every woman that ye women should not go.*[90]

Although Johnson was at first hesitant to dismiss the wives and women actually performing honest work for his army, General Lyman's advice was taken as the council of war approved the motion. On August 23, all the women in the camp were sent back to Albany, and according to John Burk, "When they went off there was a great huzza."[91] With that situation taken care of, the time was approaching for the army to begin its movement toward Lake George, where it would proceed north from there and encounter the French at Crown Point. There was already word arriving in camp that upward of six thousand enemy troops were in the Crown Point vicinity, and Johnson believed he needed more men. Only sixty Mohawks were present in his camp, and Hendrick and the rest of the promised warriors were nowhere to be found. Blanchard's New Hampshire men back at Albany were ordered forward to Fort Lyman. If the reports of the enemy's numbers were true, Johnson's force may have been too small to capture the French fortification. Writing to the royal governors whose colony's men were taking part in the expedition, Johnson laid out his plan for defending the southern end of Lake George should unwanted circumstances impede his mission:

> *The Road is now making from this place to Lake St. Sacrament* [Lake George] *where I propose to build Magazines & raise a defensible Fortification either as a safe Retreat in case we should fine the Enemy to*[o] *Strong for our Force & be obliged to quit our ground or upon well grounded Intelligence find it the most prudent Measu*[r]*e to halt there till we receive reinforcements.*[92]

He then went on in the same letter to give the governors an understanding of his army's and his own devotion to king and country:

As I think the Troops under my Command both officers & Men seem to be animated with becoming Resolution & Courage, I hope they will approve themselves in all respects worthy of the Confidence which their Country hath reposed in them and I shall endeavour to the utmost of my abilities to fulfill the Duties of that Station in which I am placed....We are engaged in a Righteous and a Glorious Cause and as far as Courage ought to carry Men I hope it will carry us. [93]

On August 26, Johnson and fifteen hundred men set out from Fort Lyman and began the final leg of their journey to the lake. Upon its arrival the army was to begin construction of docks, storehouses and fortifications along the southern shore of the lake. This was determined to be the new fallback point, not Albany, for the time being if the campaign against Crown Point did not yield favorable results. The road to the lake was cleared as the column progressed northward, and by August 28 Johnson's division arrived at its destination around four o'clock in the afternoon. The commanding general christened the previously named Lac du St. Sacrament Lake George in honor of His Royal Majesty.

While the southern shore of Lake George was transformed into an army encampment, Baron de Dieskau and his force of thirty-five hundred French Regulars, Canadians and Indians sat at Fort St. Frédéric preparing to launch their offensive. Following the victory over Braddock's army in July, soldiers from Fort Duquesne discovered among the British dead a copy of the plans for the 1755 campaigns. The document immediately made its way to Montreal, where it was reviewed by Vaudreuil. The marquis observed that Johnson's army at Albany that was set to assault Fort St. Frédéric was more of a threat than Shirley's force assembling at the dilapidated Fort Oswego. While it was important to rid all British influence from Lake Ontario, the tiny garrison of five hundred men at Crown Point would stand no chance against Johnson's superior numbers. Fort St. Frédéric was a thorn in the side of the British colonies and England's plan to claim North America—it defended the major water highway of Lake Champlain and served as a base of operations for future raids into New York's interior. Because of this, Dieskau's orders to march to Lake Ontario and attack Oswego were recalled, and he took his army to Crown Point with the new goal of defeating Johnson.

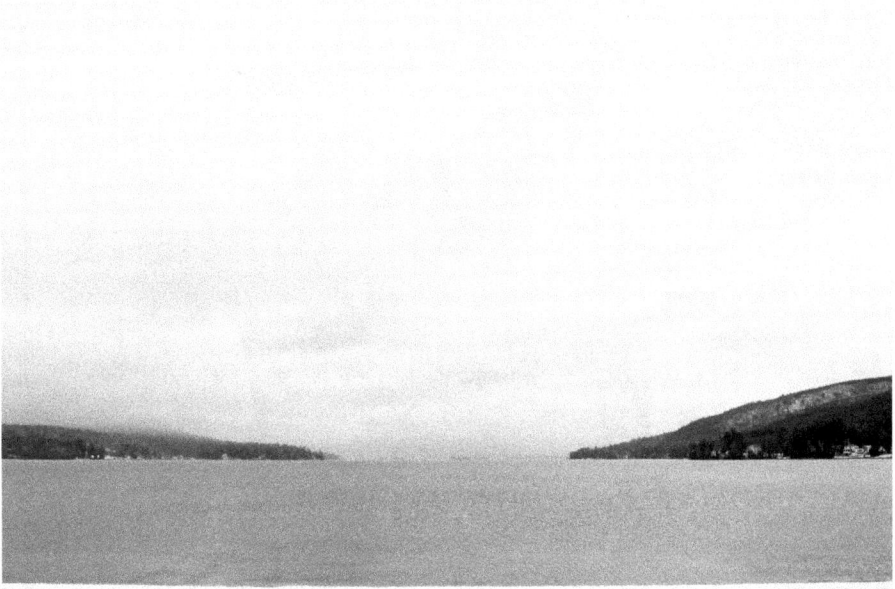

View of the southern portion of Lake George from the position of Johnson's encampment. *Author's collection.*

On August 16, Dieskau arrived at Fort St. Frédéric. Marching from Montreal in three columns, a portion of his army had preceded his contingent's arrival, and the final body marched into camp on August 20. Once he established his headquarters at Crown Point, the commanding general counted roughly 550 men garrisoning the fort and encamped within its vicinity, 1,011 regulars of the Regiments de Languedoc and La Reine, 1,412 Canadians and 600 Indians. During the army's two-week stay along Lake Champlain, Dieskau complained ruthlessly about his Indian allies. "I encountered nothing but difficulties from the Indians," the general later wrote. "Never was I able to obtain a faithful scout; at one time they refused to make any; at another time, seeming to obey me, they set forth...and return[ed] within a few days without bringing me any intelligence." Because of this, the Canadians were his only source of information, and on August 27, one came back from a reconnaissance mission with word that "3000 English were encamped at [Fort Lyman] where they were constructing a fort that was already pretty well advanced." It was not news to Dieskau that Johnson's army would be marching north from Albany, but the prospect of facing a force of nearly equal strength would have made things more difficult. However, the general had full

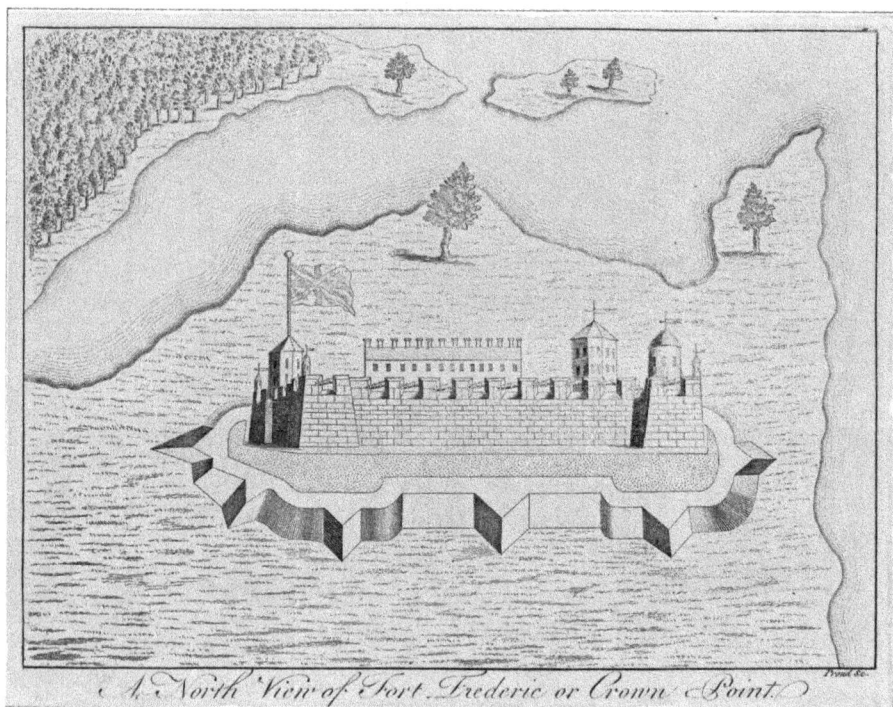

A North View of Fort Frederic or Crown Point.

Fort St. Frédéric. *Courtesy of New York Public Library Digital Collections.*

confidence in the ability of his professionally trained regulars even if he could not fully rely on the Indians.[94]

Several days before the intelligence came in regarding what was developing around Fort Lyman, marching orders were distributed to each command. The army was to march in three columns with the regular regiments in the center guarded on both flanks and front by the Canadians and Indians. Well aware of the importance of utilizing his irregular troops to fight in the wilderness of New York, especially when engaging the enemy on broken terrain, Dieskau ordered Jacques Legardeur de St. Pierre to "fight the enemy in the woods…[and] attack with the greatest force." When in combat the St. Pierre's warriors were to work in concert with the Canadian militia on the flanks, while the regulars took the fight to the enemy in the center. On September 1, the army moved out in its designated column formation and arrived the next day at Carillon. If Johnson's force was to advance any farther northward, Dieskau was determined to meet it on the field of battle before it could reach Crown Point.[95]

While the French made preparations for a counteroffensive, the provincial army was still arriving at the southern shore of the lake. On August 30, Johnson's friend Hendrick and 160 to 170 of his Mohawk warriors came into camp and were welcomed with a round of musketry by the New Englanders and New Yorkers. "Our Indians appear to be very sincere and zealous in our cause," the general wrote to the Lords of Trade in London, "and their young Men can hardly be withheld from going out a Scalping." More arrived during the next few days, and on the third, Lyman and Moses Titcomb marched into camp with the remainder of the army; several companies of the First New York Regiment stayed behind at Fort Lyman to await the arrival of Blanchard's New Hampshire men and to complete construction of the fort. The army at Lake George now counted roughly three thousand men. William Eyre was ordered to begin planning the construction of a wooden fort, and work began to construct docks and boats along the shoreline as the army's bateaux were brought up from near Fort Lyman. For months the northern colonies had been militarizing for the campaign to finally rid New York of all Frenchmen encroaching on land belonging to King George II. Now the time had come to begin the final thrust down Lake George toward Crown Point.[96]

THE BLOODY MORNING SCOUT

*F*or two days the French army milled about the heights of Carillon, erecting fortifications, magazines and storehouses to serve as a forward base of operations. Although he had struggled to get his Indian allies to cooperate with him throughout the early weeks of his campaign, Dieskau was able to send out a scouting party of Abenaki warriors to Fort Lyman between August 29 and 30. They returned on September 4 with new intelligence that would shape the remainder of the offensive. Reaching the outskirts of the British encampments at the Great Carrying Place, the Indian scouts captured a lone soldier who wandered too far from the fortifications—most likely a member of Cockcroft's First New York Regiment. They returned with their prisoner to Carillon within a few days, and immediately the man was brought to the commanding general for interrogation.

After being threatened by the Indians if he chose not to disclose accurate intelligence, the prisoner informed Dieskau that Johnson had moved with roughly three thousand provincials and Mohawk warriors to Lake George and that the British general had "contented himself with leaving 5 [to] six hundred men at the fort for the purpose of both finishing and guarding and defending it, in case of need." He went on to give a description of the fort's defenses that had been completed and also stated that the "5 [to] six hundred men" garrisoning it were all encamped outside and would not be allowed inside until it was complete. From his memory he recalled roughly twenty-eight cannons and mortars with twenty-five more pieces being expected. Only one of these guns was actually deployed, however, and it manned the gate. Along with the construction of Fort Lyman already underway, the prisoner spoke of Johnson's men building another on the southern shore of the lake. The cooperation of the prisoner gave Dieskau the intelligence that he needed to act.[97]

With the knowledge that Fort Lyman was undermanned and that Johnson's main army body was fourteen miles away from supporting them at Lake George, Dieskau determined to take fifteen hundred handpicked men from Carillon and sail them south down Lake Champlain to attack. Leaving behind the other half of his force as a second line of defense, the general detached 216 men from the grenadier companies of the Regiments de Languedoc and La Reine, 684 Canadians and 600 Indians for the raid against the English that he was personally leading.

It was decided that rather than moving directly south down Lake George, the best route for the army advance was west down Lake Champlain and into South Bay. From there the French force would avoid the Wood Creek road originally intended to be used by Johnson's army and instead follow its own overland path of roughly thirty miles to the British position at Fort Lyman. This route was chosen in order to keep the movement concealed. Having a direct route to the camp via Lake George certainly would have meant early detection and the possibility of an engagement before Dieskau's force was fully landed or prepared.

On September 4, Dieskau and his 1,500 men departed from Carillon and sailed south, arriving at the end of South Bay the following day. Upon disembarking his strike force, Dieskau detached 120 men to guard the boats and took the rest with him south before setting up camp for the evening. The army began its overland march in earnest the next day, September 6, and proceeded ten miles before encamping for the night. When first light came, the advance continued, and by that night twenty more miles had been traversed, bringing the French to within two to three miles of Fort Lyman and within striking distance. In a matter of two days the French regulars, Canadians and Indians had completed a march of thirty miles through wilderness and over incredibly broken terrain—an incredible feat. This is a testament to the discipline of the regulars, woodland skills of the irregulars and the effectiveness of compacting the march into three columns rather than one long formation. Everything had gone according to plan thus far for Dieskau. The only thing left to do was to attack and scatter the British.[98]

Things began to fall apart that evening for Dieskau as the Indians' recurring failure to cooperate would hamper the general's plans. Following

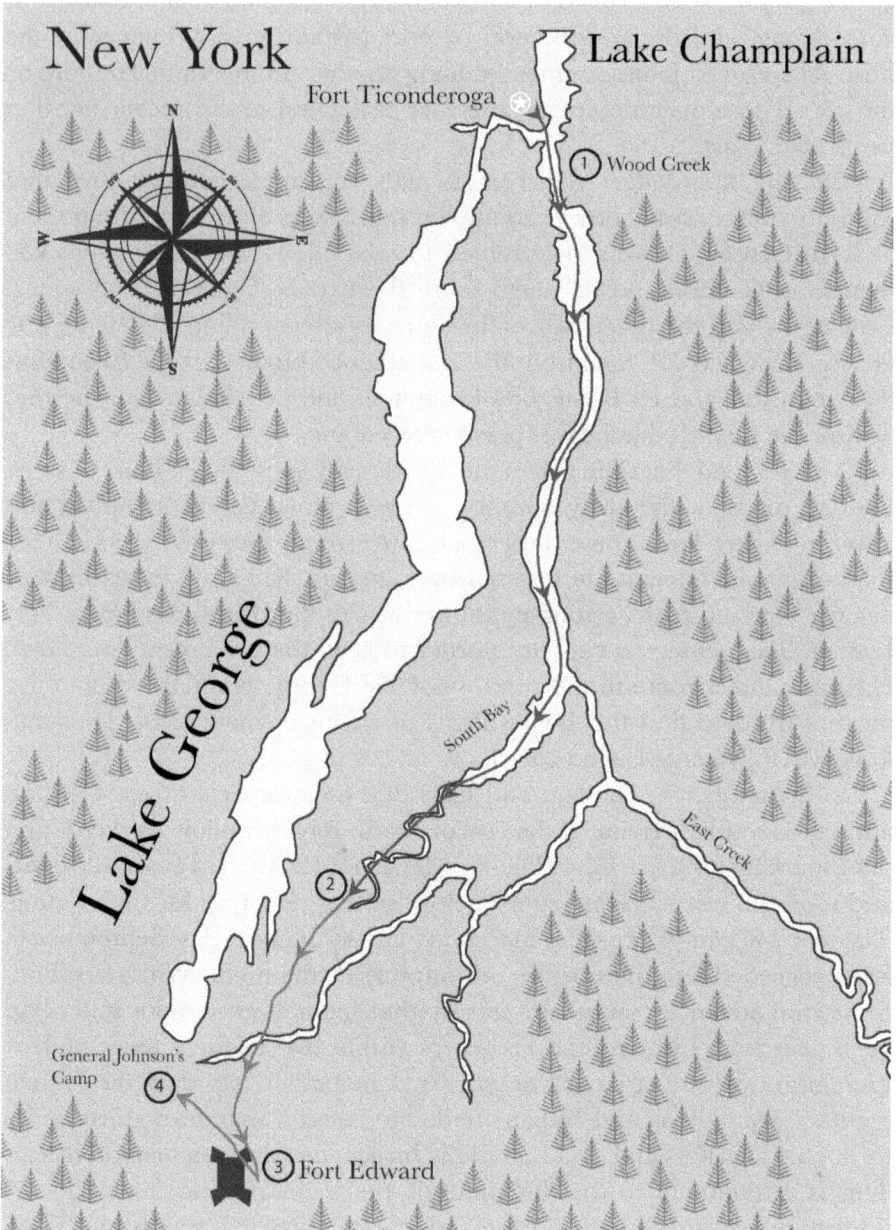

The French Path to Fort Lyman. 1) Dieskau's army departs from Carillon on September 4; 2) Dieskau's army lands at South Bay and proceeds with its march south on September 6; 3) the French army arrives several miles away from Fort Lyman on the seventh and decides to march north and attack Johnson's camp at Lake George the following day; 4) September 8, the Battle of Lake George. *Map by Nicholas Chavez.*

the arrival of the French army, scouts were sent forward to collect intelligence regarding enemy troop dispositions and strength. One of these parties shot and killed a courier coming down the military road from Johnson's camp at the lake. Discovered on the messenger's person was a dispatch intended for Colonel Joseph Blanchard at Fort Lyman, whose New Hampshire Regiment had arrived to augment the New Yorkers already there. Upon examining the letter, it was discovered that Johnson was well aware of the French landing at South Bay and was planning to send reinforcements to Fort Lyman the following day to strengthen the garrison. The newly discovered threat did not deter Dieskau from carrying out his raid. "[My assault] was a combined movement," the French general wrote a week later. "I was to arrive at nightfall at the fort and rush to the attack."

As the army advanced through the dark wilderness to launch its quick and daring raid, the columns became lost in the woods before reaching its intended target. The movement was led in large part by Caughnawaga and, according to Dieskau, "caused a wrong direction to be taken." Seemingly in an outrage upon learning of the grave mistake made by his allies, Dieskau called off the attack and immediately ordered a council of war to see if the problem could be reversed. The meeting was a disaster for the French general and strengthened his remorse for his Indian allies. When the idea was pitched to renew the assault, the Indian representatives at the council balked. Seemingly out of nowhere they refused to attack Fort Lyman. Their reasoning varied. Some believed the land on which the fort stood rightfully belonged to England and it was not their business to take it, and others simply were not warm to the idea of attacking a fort defended by infantry and artillery. In the end Dieskau had no other choice but to give in to his allies' demands; he knew very well that their assistance was crucial to obtaining victory.

The intelligence gathered from the captured dispatch earlier that evening gave the French another option. The provincials at Lake George still believed that Dieskau's army from Crown Point and Carillon numbered upward of six thousand men. There was no way for them to have obtained any accurate reports regarding the split of his own force and the numerical advantage that the British held. Because of this, it was still possible to launch a surprise attack on Johnson's encampment; seizing the initiative might very well have been enough to carry his men to victory. Both ideas were presented and a vote was held. The Indians cast their vote in favor of assaulting Johnson's camp, and preparations were made to march the following day and assume the offensive.[99]

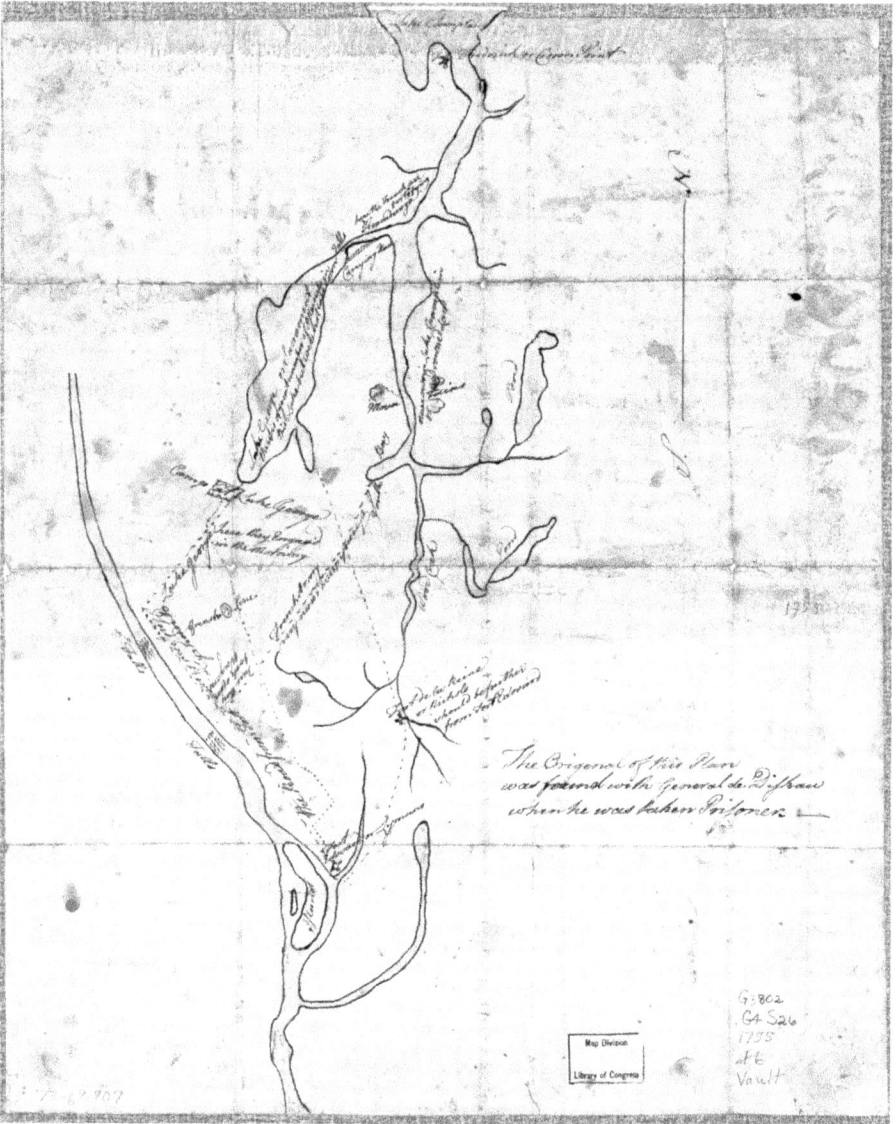

Dieskau's Map of Lake Champlain and Lake George. *Courtesy of Library of Congress.*

Earlier that day along the southern shore of Lake George, Johnson's army stirred with the sights and sounds of camp life. Men milled about on scouting and picket duties, split wood for fires, cleaned their weapons, continued construction of the storehouses and cleared the woods surrounding the camp. As the enlisted men kept busy, so, too, did the officers. That afternoon a council of war was held in which each regiments' commander attended. The topic of discussion was the size of the fort that was to be built on the ground that the army occupied. Johnson was a firm believer that a larger fort should be built that could "be maintained even against some Artillery [which] was very necessary not only to secure a Retreat to the present Forces in case of Necessity, but to maintain the possession of [H]is Majesty's Title to this important pass for the time to come." Much to Johnson's displeasure, the other officers felt it was more practical to erect a "Picketted Fort" that could accommodate one hundred men. This task could be completed much quicker than a full-size fortification and would not require Johnson to detach a great number of men to construct it, thus not terribly impeding the progress of the campaign. Planned and laid out by Captain Eyre, construction of the fort was given to Ephraim Williams and the Third Massachusetts Regiment.[100]

The debate over the size of the Lake George fort would have to be placed on the back burner, however, because around four o'clock that afternoon a group of Mohawk scouts returned to camp with some disturbing news. They had ventured to South Bay several days before and uncovered tracks leading from the shoreline. Upon further investigation even more were discovered, and the sound of sporadic musket discharges could be distantly heard through the peaceful wilderness. The warriors originally assumed that if the French army was near it most certainly was marching via the Wood Creek road. Traveling a short distance down the path, the Mohawks could not find any evidence of a moving body of troops. When they turned back to return to South Bay, they stumbled upon three hastily built roads through the woods—the same ones used by Dieskau's columns probably only the day before. This was enough information for Johnson to raise the alarm. It was obvious that Dieskau was moving on Fort Lyman, although with how large a force was not known. Johnson quickly acted and had his secretary, Peter Wraxall, scribble off a warning message to Joseph Blanchard at Fort Lyman. It was critical for the dispatch to be delivered at that very moment, and Johnson searched for a volunteer to ride post-haste through the night. After none of the New Englanders stepped forward, a brave New York wagoner, Jacob Adams, answered the general's call.[101]

Adams mounted a horse given to him by Johnson and exited the camp, riding full-speed down the military road and off into the unforgiving Adirondack wilderness. He galloped as fast as his animal would allow and made it to within roughly two miles of Fort Lyman when, according to Lieutenant Daniel Claus—somewhat of an adopted son of Johnson's who had lived with the general prior to the war and now served as part of his Indian Affairs office—he "found himself in the Midst of the French Army & was called to stop." Determined to break through the enemy lines, Adams ignored the threat surrounding him and pushed forward until he was "fired at, knocked off the horse & the Dispatches found upon him." Around midnight, news of Adams's demise made its way into Johnson's camp when a party of two soldiers and two Mohawks who had been sent on foot with the same letter returned with a captured wagoner who had stolen from the camp and attempted to make a run for it before being caught. The wagoner claimed that he had "heard and saw the Enemy about 4 miles from this side [of] the Carrying Place; they heard a Gun fire, and a man Call upon Heaven for Mercy, which he Judged to be Adams." It was clear that Johnson's courier was dead and that the orders for Blanchard that he carried had fallen into enemy hands. Cockcroft's and Blanchard's men were in danger of being surprised and overwhelmed by the French if help could not be sent. Early the next morning, September 8, 1755, Johnson once again called a council of war so the situation could be reassessed and the necessary measures made to reinforce or possibly relieve the garrison at Fort Lyman should it be besieged or attacked.[102]

As the sun began to rise over the eastern mountains and shine its morning rays along the rippling waters of Lake George, Johnson and his subordinates knew that time was of the essence. Every moment spent debating what to do next was one that could be used to send Blanchard assistance. At first a plan was devised to send two columns out on the march in different directions. The first would be commanded by Ephraim Williams and consist of his own Third Massachusetts Regiment. They were to immediately march south to Fort Lyman. A second column made up of Nathan Whiting and his Second Connecticut was tasked with advancing to South Bay and seizing the boats left behind by the French to make their only avenue of retreat north to Carillon overland. Disagreeing with the whole premise of splitting a force into two, Chief Hendrick stepped forward with a bundle of sticks and demonstrated that it was easy to break them individually, but not if they were held together. The message was received, and Whiting was ordered to march with Williams, to the relief of Fort Lyman. Hendrick would accompany them with roughly two hundred of his warriors and lead the advance.[103]

As the men of the Second Connecticut and Third Massachusetts broke camp that morning and prepared to fall into columns along the military road, Captain Elisha Hawley penned the final words in a letter to his brother back home in Northampton: "I am this minute a going out in Company with five hundred men [of the Third Massachusetts] to see if we can Intercept [the French] in their retreat…and therefore must conclude this letter." As he folded the letter and stored it for a later sending, Captain Hawley, twenty-nine years old on September 8, was full of life and ready to meet the French in the field and defeat them for king and country. He probably did not have the slightest thought in his mind that he would never see his brother again. So many men that day who fell into column and made ready to march were destined to witness firsthand one of the most infamous events in New England's colonial history.[104]

The single column of twelve hundred men was put into motion around eight o'clock in the morning. Hendrick's Mohawks led the way with their fearless veteran leader mounted atop his horse at the head. They moved in a single file, while the New Englanders followed marching in files of five or six men across. The advance south was anticlimactic at the onset, and Williams ordered a halt roughly a mile and a half from the camp to allow the Connecticut men to close the gap between them and his regiment. It was at this time that flanking parties were sent out to scan the surrounding woods at least until Whiting caught up—whether or not they remained on the flanks when the march resumed is somewhat of a mystery, just as many of the events that would transpire that morning are today. While the Mohawk and Massachusetts men stood halted along the road, a scurry of frightened animals broke out of the wilderness to the front of the column. Nothing significant followed behind them, but to add to the immense folklore that was born that morning, Hendrick, who was conferring with Williams at the time, supposedly in a prophetic tone turned to the colonel and exclaimed, "I smell Indians." The great warrior rode back to the head of the column, and as Whiting's men came up behind the Third Massachusetts, the march recommenced.[105]

Several miles up the road the woods were astir with movement. Around ten o'clock scouts returned to Baron de Dieskau, who had set his army in motion early that morning and informed the general and his second-in-command, Pierre-André Gohin, Comte de Montreuil, that they had "seen a large body of troops on their way to the fort." Shortly after, some English prisoners were brought in and reaffirmed the reports made by the scouts. Early twentieth-century Ephraim Williams biographer William Andrews Pew argued that these prisoners were evidence that the provincial and Mohawk column had indeed sent out flankers or at least a forward reconnaissance party ahead of the men. This is possible, but the captured Englishmen could also have been deserters from the camp or some more waggoneers trying to make a break for it with stolen goods. Regardless of the scenario, Dieskau determined to spring a trap for the men coming to reinforce Fort Lyman. He ordered his army forward in its three-column formation with the Canadians on the right, the regulars in the center and St. Pierre and his Indians on the left.[106]

Dieskau's army was still following his strict marching orders from the end of August before it departed from Crown Point. Under these orders, the general made it very clear that once the army became engaged in battle with the enemy:

> All troops in general, Indians and others, are warned not to amuse themselves pillaging during the battle, and to follow the enemy as far as possible, and the camp will be pillaged as soon as the fight will be entirely concluded. Monsieur de Saint Pierre will have the goodness to make the Indians understand reason on that point, especially not to amuse themselves scalping until the enemy is entirely defeated, inasmuch as ten men can be killed whilst one is being scalped. I expect this obedience from my children.[107]

The battle that was about to take place that morning would be the Indians' first test of obedience. Under St. Pierre's watchful eye and ability, they were in good hands.

Dieskau's army took its position overlooking either side of the road and across it between three and four miles from Johnson's encampment. The Indians lined the west side of the road, extending much farther north than the Canadians on the east side. The natives, according to sutler Samuel Blodget, who interviewed participants following the battle, occupied "a continued Eminence filled with Rocks, and Trees, and Shrubs as high as a Man's Breast," and their line extended for a half mile or so. The Canadian position was much smaller in length and was masked by a thick growth of brush and trees. The grenadiers deployed across the road farther to the south. When completed, the deployment resembled a hook, or a cul de sac. The plan was simple: Wait for the enemy column to come within musket range of the regulars and do not fire until the grenadiers initiated the battle. Dieskau's army waited patiently and in complete silence for the enemy to venture into its trap.[108]

Around 10:30 a.m., the British column had ventured a little over three miles from camp when it slowly began to make its way into the French ambush site. What happened next is widely debated, and all primary sources regarding the incident are by word of mouth. Apparently, a noise was

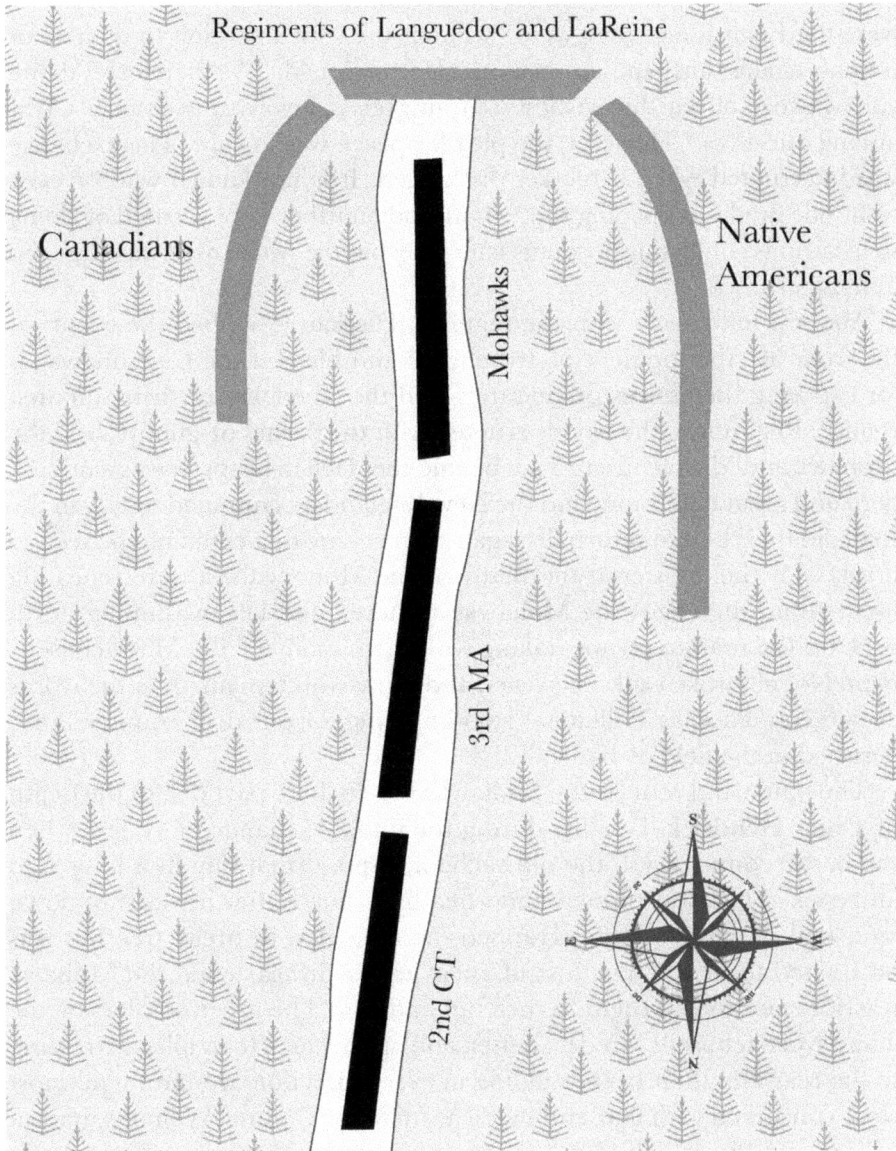

Regiments of Languedoc and LaReine

Canadians

Native Americans

Mohawks

3rd MA

2nd CT

The Bloody Morning Scout. *Map by Nicholas Chavez.*

heard from the woods to the right of the British column, which prompted Hendrick to halt. The French-allied Caughnawagas were cousins of the English Mohawks, and one of the warriors began to exchange words of warning with Hendrick. He urged the Mohawks to disperse, as their enemies were the English and they were "without the least Intention to quarrel or trespass against any [Indian] Nation." He continued, "We therefor[e] desire you will keep out of the way lest we transgress & involve ourselves in a War among ourselves." However, the plea for peace was in vain. The exchange was interrupted when a musket discharged. It is not known who or even what side fired this opening shot—both Indian tribes were accused of doing so in various conflicting accounts later on—but the whole road was engulfed in musketry.[109]

About a mile away with the regulars, Dieskau described the events at the front as "the moment of treachery" and blamed the Caughnawagas for exposing themselves prematurely and the Abenakis for firing the first rounds. Regardless, the woods erupted with the flashes of gunfire, and the Mohawk and Massachusetts men behind them fell in heaps. It was a time of peril and great confusion, and the New Englanders crammed tightly in the road did their best to return fire against an enemy that could not be seen— it was as if the disaster at the Battle of the Monongahela were repeating itself. Amid the chaos the Mohawks scattered and began running north back up the road to escape, taking with them many of the Massachusetts men. Not all broke ranks, however, and those who remained, in the words of surgeon Thomas Williams, "stood fighting for our dear country [and] perished in the field of battle."[110]

The panic and rout of the Mohawks was in large part due to the death of Chief Hendrick. Possibly during the initial exchange of volleys when the battle commenced, the old sachem, dressed that day in a long coat and cocked hat, was pinned underneath his horse after it was shot down by a hail of musket balls. Trapped, he struggled to break free but was bayoneted to death. The loss of their leader disheartened the Mohawk warriors and forced them to turn tail and run. The green soldiers of the Third Massachusetts fared no better, and upon seeing their allies retreating to the rear and their friends falling in every direction around them, most were consumed with fear and made a run for it. Colonel Williams made a valiant effort to rally his broken companies and with sword in hand made a rush up the western embankment toward the enemy. Attempting to inspire his men the old martial way, he stood atop a boulder urging them to hold the line and take the fight to the enemy. Not a moment had passed when a musket ball struck Williams in the head, killing him instantly. Before they left the field with the rest of the regiment, a handful of loyal Bay Staters retrieved their beloved colonel's body and hid it beneath some thick brush to prevent it from being discovered by the French Indians and

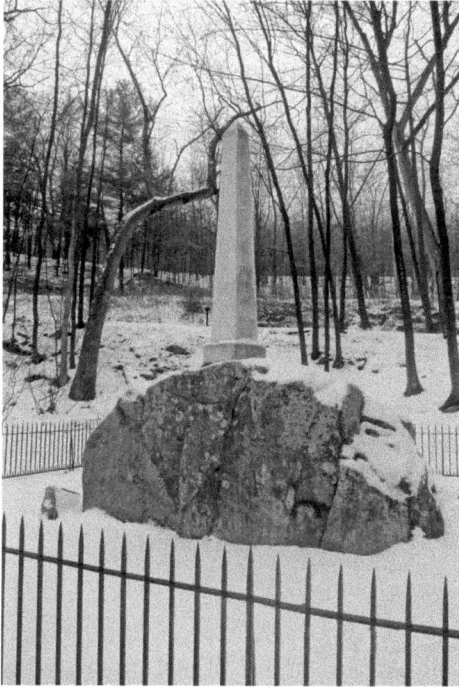

Obelisk to Ephraim Williams placed by
Williams College alumni marking the supposed
spot of his death during the Bloody Morning
Scout. *Author's collection.*

desecrated. Around the same time, Elisha Hawley received a mortal wound to the chest and was carried from the field. All unit cohesion had broken down, and the entire regiment was on the road heading north back to Johnson's camp. Only Nathan Whiting's Second Connecticut remained, poised to prevent a disastrous rout.[111]

Lieutenant Colonel Nathan Whiting and his five hundred Connecticut men were far behind at the rear of the column and not involved in the ambush. The musketry to their front and the sight of their comrades beating a hasty retreat through their own ranks must have unnerved the men just as it had done to everyone else that terrible morning. Something needed to be done, however, to slow the onrushing Canadians, French-allied Indians and grenadiers whom Baron de Dieskau had pushed forward into the maelstrom. Rallying as many of the Mohawk and Massachusetts men that he possibly could, Whiting ordered them to gradually pull back and utilize every bush, stone and tree as cover to fire at the charging enemy. If he could not stand and fight, he would run and fight. The maneuver was conducted in perfect concert; as the rest of the men "fled in a disorderly Manner towards the Camp," according to Peter Wraxall, Whiting and his brave band of warriors and soldiers stood firm, loading and firing every chance they could get before falling back to the next form of concealment. It is quite possible that this was the first organized fighting retreat ever performed in America during a military engagement.[112]

For over an hour the rearguard fought its way through the wilderness back to the main encampment. To assist in the effort to extract the retreating men, Johnson sent Edward Cole and a few hundred of his First Rhode Island forward from the camp. The combined force was more than enough to hold back the onrushing French, who were losing many of their Indians along the way due to disobeying orders or a failure to cooperate and advance. It was nearing noon when the men of the fighting retreat had discharged their final blasts of musketry. They came within three quarters of a mile from Johnson's camp when they finally turned and made a run for the rest of the army. In what Seth Pomeroy described as "a very handsom[e] retre[a]t" in his journal that evening, Nathan Whiting had bought valuable time for the men at the lake—time that would prove crucial in deciding the day. The first engagement of the Battle of Lake George, forever known afterward as "the Bloody Morning Scout," was over.[113]

7

THE BATTLE OF LAKE GEORGE

When the fighting erupted down the military road around 10:30 a.m., the sound of musketry could be heard by the men with Johnson still at the Lake George encampment. It was clear that the column sent to reinforce Fort Lyman had run into trouble a lot sooner than anticipated, and the echo of gunfire inching closer to the camp was evidence enough that Williams's command was in full retreat. Preparations were hastily made to fortify the encampment. According to General Johnson, the army worked quickly to "[throw] up a Breast Work of Trees round our Encampment, and Planted [artillery] to defend the Same, [and] We Immediately [hauled] Some heavy Cannon up [to the road] to Strengthen our Front." The ground in front of the works, cleared earlier upon the army's arrival at the lake, gave them a field of fire of about one hundred yards. The defenses were anything but impregnable, but they certainly gave the provincials a sense of comfort knowing that they would not have to face the French standing up on open ground.[114]

For the next hour and a half survivors of the Bloody Morning Scout streamed through the woods south post-haste into the camp. The firing was heard less than a mile away as Whiting's fighting retreat neared the lake. Preparations were made to receive the Connecticut men and the others who had stayed and fought by their side, as well as the wounded in search of medical treatment. Captain Eyre took command of the heavy artillery guarding the entrance of the camp along the road—probably eighteen- or thirty-two-pounders—and aimed them straight at the anticipated avenue of approach of the oncoming French. It was nearing noon when Whiting's men fired their last volleys in the enemy's direction and then broke for the camp. From the provincial line the French were "Se[e]n to Drop as Pig[e]ons," according to Seth Pomeroy, but it did not deter them from driving forward with an "u[n]da[u]nted Co[u]rage." The last of the retreating Mohawks and New Englanders made their way over the breastworks, and for a moment the guns fell silent.[115]

With the small lull in the fighting, Johnson and Lyman finished the deployment of their defensive line. According to the personal journal of historian Francis Parkman, who visited the site of the battle in 1878, "Johnson's position seems to have been about 300 yards from the lake, between the hill [on the left] & an extensive swampy hollow...on the right, his front being not more than 150 to 200 yards." When the entire line was in place, the regimental dispositions from left to right were as follows: Fitch's Connecticut companies of the First New York Regiment, First Connecticut, Second Connecticut and the First, Second and Third Massachusetts Regiments on the right. It is not exactly clear where Cole's First Rhode Island was positioned, but since it was among the last to return to the camp

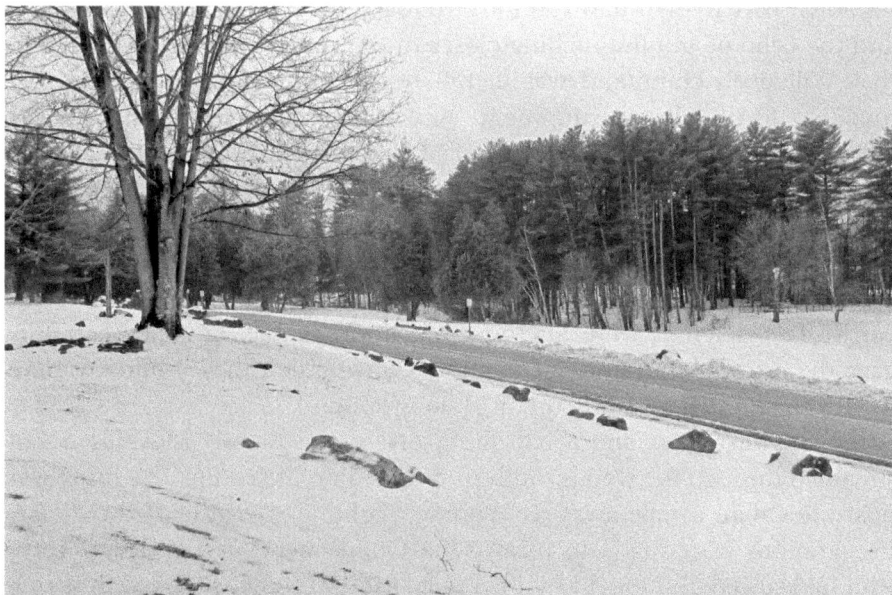

Modern-day view looking southwest of the park road that follows the original military road, Lake George Battlefield Park. It was near this position that William Eyre deployed his heavy cannons. *Author's collection.*

after being sent forward to assist Whiting during his fighting retreat, it is possible that it was divided up and placed on the flanks as guards or held in reserve. Eyre posted the three heavy guns in the road splitting the two Connecticut regiments and a fourth on the left between the Second Connecticut and the First New York.[116]

About half a mile from the provincial line, Dieskau halted his command in order for them to regroup and redeploy for the next attack. His army had pursued the enemy for over three miles and must have been showing some signs of fatigue. Regardless, the general knew that the only way to force the British from their defenses was to seize the initiative and strike fast. "Monsieur de Dieskau," in the words of Montreuil, "seeing the camp quite close, ordered 220 men belonging to La Reine and Languedoc regiments, to charge with fixed bayonets." As the grenadiers deployed in a compact line of battle meant to work as a sledgehammer and slam through the provincial defenses—eyewitness accounts state it was a formation six ranks deep—the Indians and Canadians veered off to the left and took their positions in the woods poised to make an attack in their "own fashion." It was now past noon and the regulars began their advance.[117]

The sight of these gray-clad professional European soldiers charging forward left many of the provincials in awe. "Their arms," Phineas Lyman poetically remembered, "glistened like the sun with their bayonets fixed and as confident, I suppose of coming straight into our camp and carrying all before them as ever an army was." The imposing spectacle, he feared, however, would shake his men and force them to "run as Braddock's did." To combat this and raise morale, the general roamed about, "encouraging them by all arts I was master of for there was no other officer to help do the same." He gathered survivors of the morning's fight and threw them into the ranks and threatened to kill all who refused to fight like men. His frustration toward the field officers and the enlisted men grew, and with a bit of humor he later lamented that their "commands did not influence them any more than the trees." For nearly all who picked up a musket in the provincial camp that day, this was their first taste of true combat. Soon enough the chaos of battle and the horrors of war would be made clear to them and be forever etched in their memory.[118]

The men of the Languedoc and La Reine Regiments advanced defiantly down the military road toward the provincial defenses. Behind the breastwork of fallen trees, General Johnson rode with Peter Wraxall, doing all in his "Power to animate our people." Halting slightly out of musket range, the grenadiers let loose a volley of musketry, firing by platoon. Their

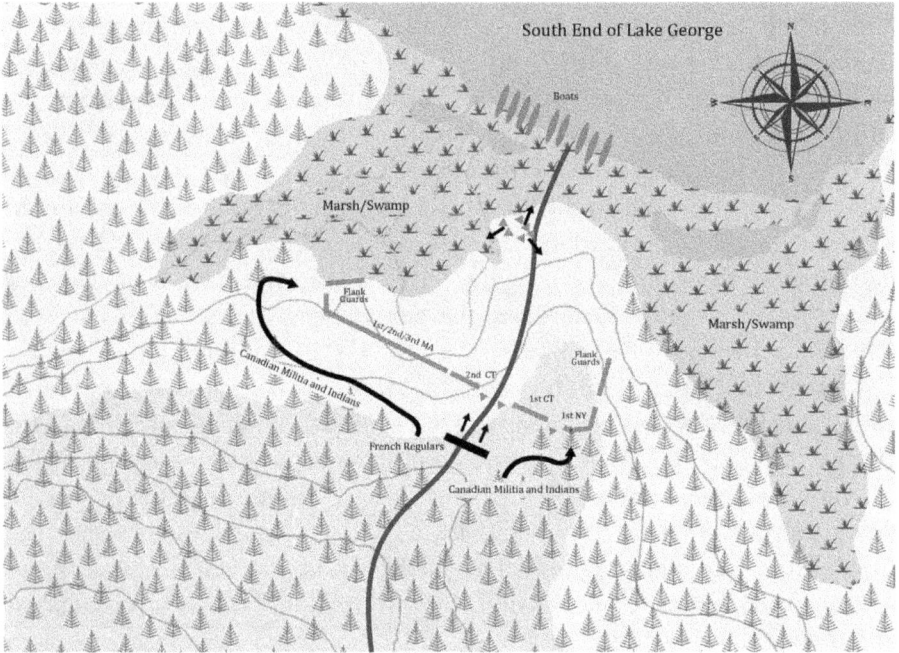

The main engagement of the Battle of Lake George. Note: The dispositions of Cole's First Rhode Island Regiment are not known. It is possible that they were used on both flanks or simply held in reserve. *Map by Nicholas Chavez.*

effect was minimal, and the colonials answered back with a volley of their own and several rounds of solid shot from Eyre's guns, which cut "Lanes, Streets and Alleys thro' their army" and forced the regulars to seek cover in the woods. The sight of artillery and well-defended breastworks caused the Indians to lose their nerves. They were already taken aback by the fact that Johnson's army contained Mohawks, with whom they wished not to engage in battle, and their leader, Legardeur de St. Pierre, had been killed during the morning's fight, so there was no real command structure above them. They hid in the woods and fired at the camp from behind rocks and trees but refused to move forward when Dieskau called on them to attack across the clearing. Seeing their fellow irregulars adamant about fighting behind cover, the Canadians determined to stand pat as well. Dieskau's luck was running out. If he intended to force the provincials from their defenses, he would have to do so with only his regulars.[119]

At the outbreak of the fighting William Johnson was wounded when a musket ball struck him in the buttocks. A painful wound, it was not serious, but the general retired to his tent for the time being for minor medical treatment. Thus, Phineas Lyman was given command of the battle. "There was in a minute nothing but the continual clangor of cannon and small arms which held for a long time," Lyman wrote in a letter to his wife. "I saw our men shoot so fast and some of them so carelessly that I was afraid the enemy intended to draw our shot . . . and break in upon us." In order to prevent the men from expending too much ammunition so early in the fight and from fouling their weapons, Lyman "[ran] from one end of the firing to the other and halloo[ed] as loud as I could speak to some of them to save their fire." Many obeyed his command. "Never men nor mortals fought better in the world," he proudly proclaimed.[120]

Not all of the men behaved as well as the ones Lyman spoke of. After Johnson's wounding, Peter Wraxall remained at the front performing the general's work of encouraging the men. Making his way across the line, Wraxall noted, "Great Numbers of our men hid themselves . . . and many pretended Sickness." He tried to force some of the pretenders to the frontline, but "for the most Part in vain." With or without the cowards the fighting continued as the French Regulars tried repeatedly to break the center of the provincial line. The Connecticut men deployed astride the

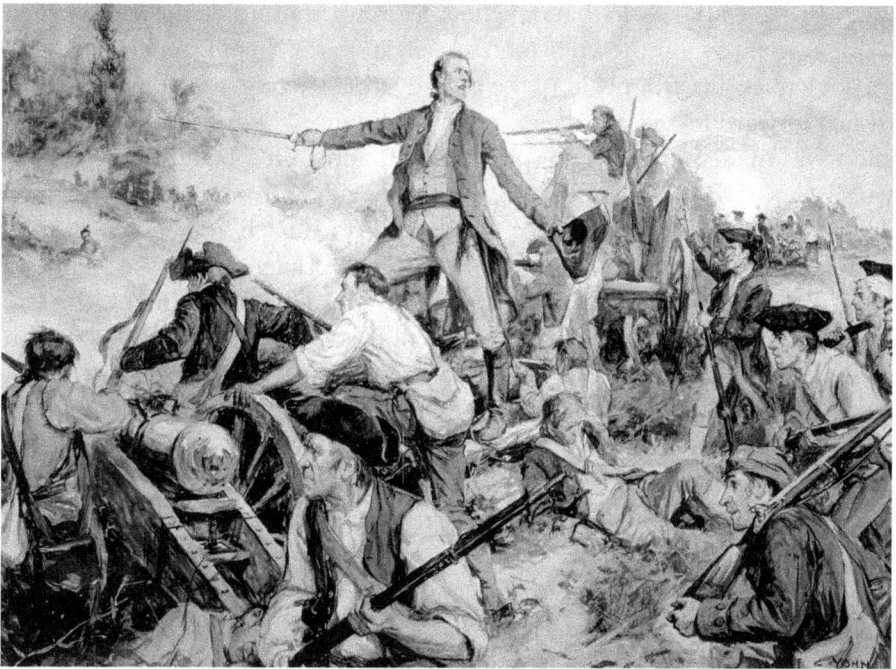

The Battle of Lake George by Frederick Coffay Yohn, 1905. *Author's collection.*

road bore the brunt of the initial attack. Eyre's cannons continued their work, forcing the French line to waver back and forth, and whenever the gray coats of Languedoc and La Reine advanced within musket range, the New Englanders discharged their Short Lands and trade guns into their enemy's front. For two hours attacks on the provincial center came. The repeated charges against the camp did nothing but produce more casualties among the regulars' ranks. "The enemy's musketry produced considerable effect," Montreuil admitted, "which threw the detachment into confusion." In Dieskau's own words, "The Regulars received the whole of the enemy's fire and perished there almost to a man." Recognizing that no significant progress was being made with the present plan, Dieskau looked to his left and determined to shift the assault.[121]

Around two o'clock in the afternoon the fighting veered toward the right of the provincial line where the First, Second and Third Massachusetts Regiments were deployed. Since the onset of the battle they had been occupied with the Canadians and Indians to their front, taking cover and sniping from the tree line. Now they were faced with throwing back the grenadiers who "Maintained a very Warm fire" against Moses Titcomb's men on the right of the line. Eyre directed his guns toward the new threat and threw some thirty-two-pound balls in that direction. Mortars from inside the camp joined in the fray, and soon the French attack began to stall again. As his men kept up a relentless fire from behind the breastworks, Titcomb and another officer rushed forward to "a large Tree…a Rod's Distance" in front of the line. The effort was made in order to inspire the men and gain a better position from which to fire. Both Titcomb and the lieutenant were immediately gunned down and killed. He was the second colonel to die in action that day.[122]

Behind the lines, the surgeons were hard at work tending to the wounded being brought in from the front by the dozens. Thomas Williams, the late Ephraim Williams's brother and regimental doctor, left a vivid description of his experiences that day while performing his medical duties under fire:

> The wounded were brought in very fast, & it was with the utmost difficulty that their wounds could be dressed fast enough, even in the most superficial manner, having in about three hours near forty men to be dressed, & Dr. Pynchon, his mate & Billy (one of his students) & myself were all to do it, my mate being at Fort Lyman attending upon divers[e] sick men there. The bullets flew like hail-stones about our ears all the time of dressing, as we had not a place prepared for safety, to dress the wounded in, but through God's goodness we received no hurt any more than the bark of the trees &

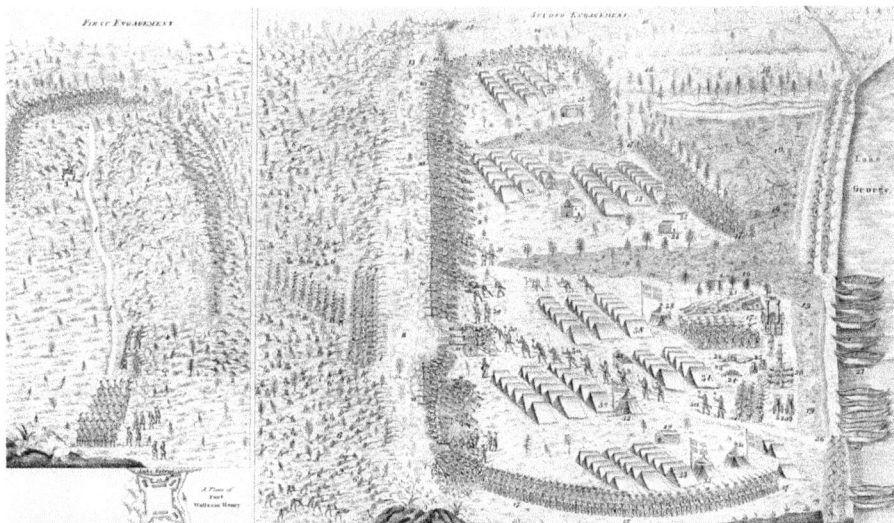

Samuel Blodget's *The Battle Near Lake George in 1755, a Prospective Plan* (London, 1756).

*chips flying in our faces by accidental shots, which we thought best to leave
& retire a few rods behind a shelter of a log house, which [was] so loose
as to let the balls through very often.*[123]

As the French Regulars traded shots with the Massachusetts men and
the surgeons tended to the wounded, Dieskau and Montreuil attempted
to gather the Canadians and Indians to press them forward against the
provincial flank. To their despair they discovered that many of the irregulars
had left the field and either returned to the morning's battlefield to pillage
and scalp or had seen more than enough fighting for their liking and began
heading home. It was well past three o'clock in the afternoon, and all hope
of seizing the English camp began to appear bleak. The French fire began to
slacken, and Dieskau determined to push the attack forward once more. He
exposed himself in the clearing while attempting to lead the assault and was
wounded in the leg. He fell to the ground in pain and then propped himself
up against a tree when an onrushing Montreuil came to his aid. "He insisted
on staying on the same spot," Montreuil said of his commanding general. "I
had no sooner washed his wound with brandy, than he received another ball
in the right knee and hip." In an effort to remove the wounded Dieskau from
the dangerous spot, Montreuil called for two Canadians to help carry him
to the rear. One of them was killed, and Dieskau insisted that the two men
leave him and get to safety. He then ordered Montreuil to find the regulars

and rally them for another attack. The lieutenant colonel reluctantly agreed to leave the general and went to seek out the grenadiers in the woods.[124]

When Montreuil located the regulars, it was too late to organize another assault. "As I was approaching the troop, it had just wheeled right about, in order to retire," he remembered. "I was obliged to take the command, and to stop the disorder as well as I was able." It was for naught. With nearly all of the Canadians and Indians already gone or falling back farther from the battlefield, the regulars were on their own and nearly fought out. Seeing the enemy retreat commencing, Mohawks from inside Johnson's camp rushed over the breastworks and charged with tomahawks into the field. Many provincials followed suit and pursued the French for a few hundred yards before returning to the camp. "They retreated in sad disorder," an artilleryman with William Eyre jeered, "and with shouts of Victory we got the day." The lake was secure for now, and the provincials had won themselves the field.[125]

It was around four o'clock in the afternoon when the French retreated from the battlefield. Peter Wraxall called it a "fortunate Repulse" and felt that the army should not occupy itself with pursuing the enemy any farther than it already had. It was only a few hours away from becoming dark, and it was not known whether or not any French reinforcements were in the area. The men were tired—both mentally and physically—and had done enough fighting for one day. There were other matters to attend to: the wounded needed to be treated, and the prisoners taken needed to be rounded up and questioned to gather intelligence. One of those prisoners brought into camp was Baron de Dieskau. Around six o'clock the French general was taken to Johnson's tent, where he was still having his wound dressed. Dieskau was well received, and Johnson treated him as a guest rather than an enemy. Johnson insisted that the baron be treated first as his wounds were much more serious—Dieskau had received a fourth wound when a New Englander trying to make him his prisoner shot him through the bladder for fear that he may have been carrying a weapon. "Le Baron de Dieskau," William Johnson wrote of his counterpart, "is an Elderly Gentlemen, an Experienced Officer, and a man of high Consideration in France." While receiving medical attention, the French general's life was threatened by a group of Mohawks who desired him dead. After a lengthy conversation with Johnson, they were persuaded otherwise and entered the tent to exchange pleasantries. Guards remained posted at the entrance for the remainder of the evening.[126]

As the sun set over the western mountains, the army prepared supper and discussed the experiences from that day. The battle was not over yet,

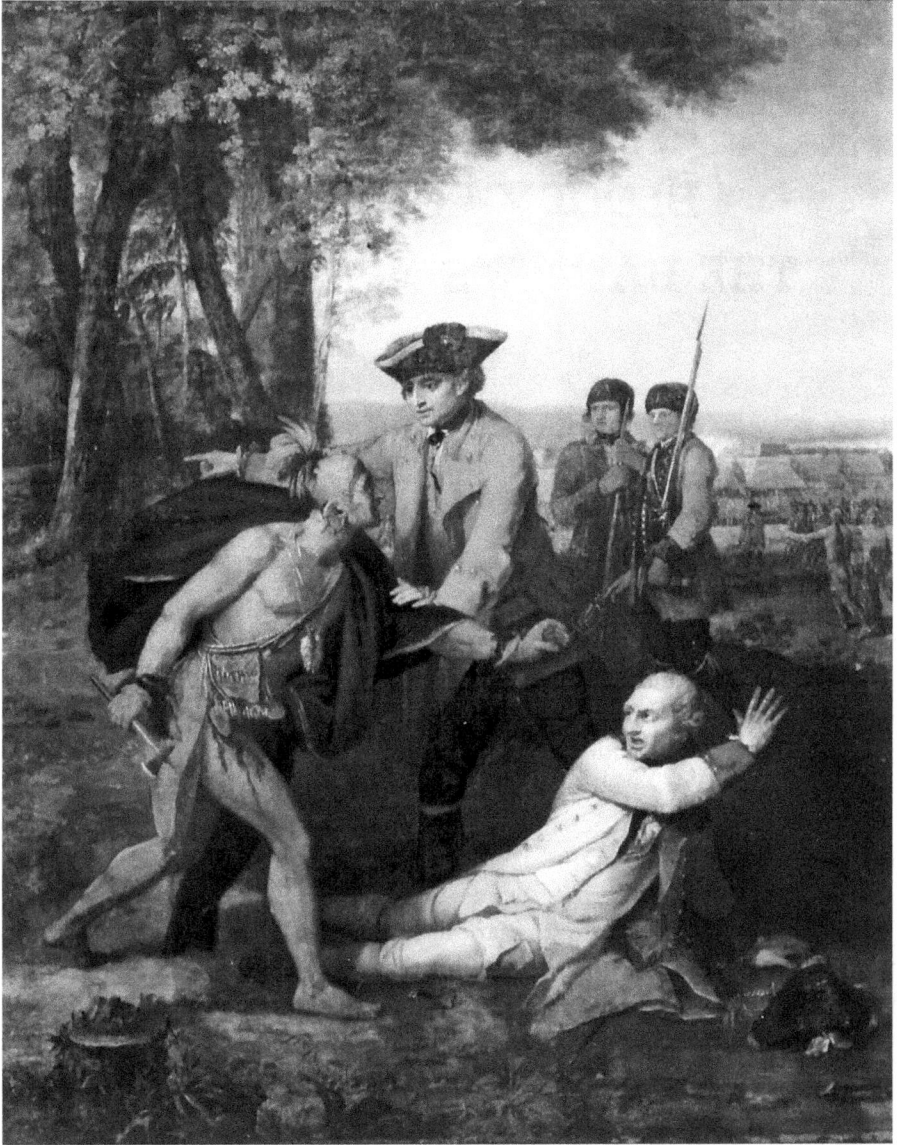

General Johnson Saving a Wounded French Officer from the Tomahawk of a North American Indian by Benjamin West, 1768. *Author's collection.*

however. In fact, the bloodiest engagement of the day had yet to take place. Several miles to the south near the morning's battlefield, several hundred provincials who had made their way from Fort Lyman leveled their muskets and took aim at an unsuspecting enemy.

8

BLOODY POND AND
THE BATTLE'S AFTERMATH

*T*he rattle of musketry that resulted in the death of wagoner Jacob Adams the night before had been heard by the men at Fort Lyman. The following morning, Joseph Blanchard ordered a reconnaissance force of sixty men from his regiment under the command of Captain Nathaniel Folsom to venture outside the fort in all directions to locate the source of the gunfire. Their search yielded some horrible discoveries. The body of Adams was found "dead & scalp'd" lying along the road, and several wagons sat engulfed in flames. Around 10:30 a.m. the detachment was alerted by the sound of the Bloody Morning Scout unfolding ten or so miles to the north. Word was sent back to Fort Lyman, and the party returned until the next move could be decided. It was clear that a large body of French and Indians was in motion toward Johnson's encampment, and something needed to be done to assist the provincial army at the lake. A council of war was held at Fort Lyman following the return of Folsom's men, and it was resolved to dispatch reinforcements to the lake.[127]

Probably around noon or a little after—just as the battle was commencing at Johnson's camp, which could clearly be heard from the fort—143 men of the New Hampshire Regiment under the direction of Captain Folsom and 90 New Yorkers led by Captain William McGinnis left Fort Lyman and hustled north up the military road to gather more intelligence of the enemy's whereabouts. As the sound of musketry grew louder and more numerous near the lake, Folsom and McGinnis scrapped their orders and headed toward the battle. "This being an extraordinary case," Folsom recorded in a letter several months later, "I was not afraid of being blamed by our super[ior] officers for helping our friends in distress." They had covered twelve miles when, around five o'clock, they caught sight of roughly 300 Canadians and Indians milling about the morning's battlefield and near a small pond, resting and counting their plunder.[128]

After chasing away a few of the enemy who had ventured from the rest of the group, Folsom ordered his New Hampshire men forward and with a "loud huzza [they] followed them up a rising ground and then met a large body of French and Indians, on whom we discharg'd our guns briskly till we exchang'd shots about four or five times." Folsom ordered the New Yorkers up to assist his men, and after forty-five minutes of intense combat, the line began to waver due to fatigue. Not wanting to abandon the field in the face of the enemy, the captain and a handful of men rushed forward again and reignited the battle. The sight of the onrushing provincials was too much for the Canadians and Indians, who had been fighting all day. "Seeing us coming upon them (we [having our muskets] charg'd and they discharg'd)," Folsom remembered, "they [ran] and gave us the ground." The fighting was over, and the provincials gained possession of the morning's battlefield and the pond, into which, according to local folklore, many of the dead were dumped, staining the water red and forever giving it the name "Bloody Pond."[129]

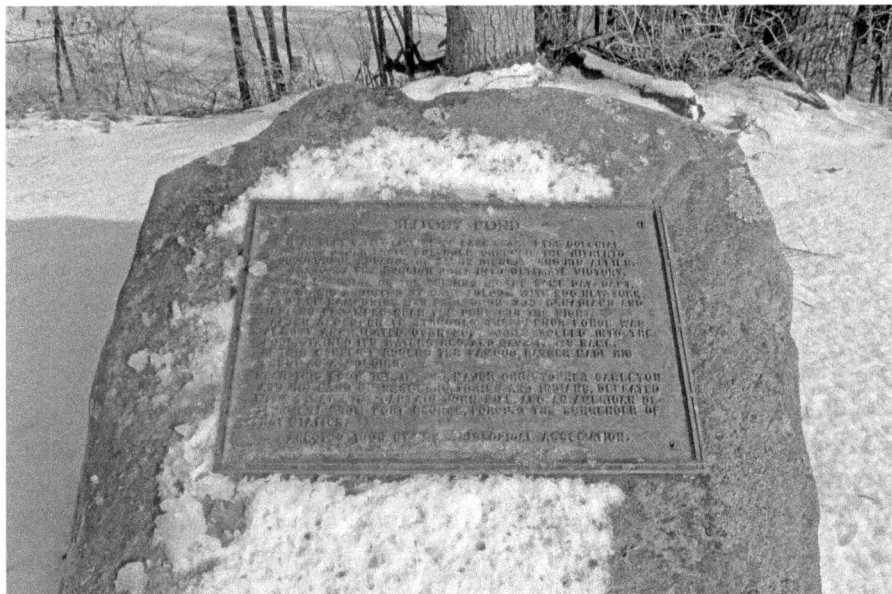

Detailed view of a historic tablet marking the site of the supposed Bloody Pond. *Author's collection.*

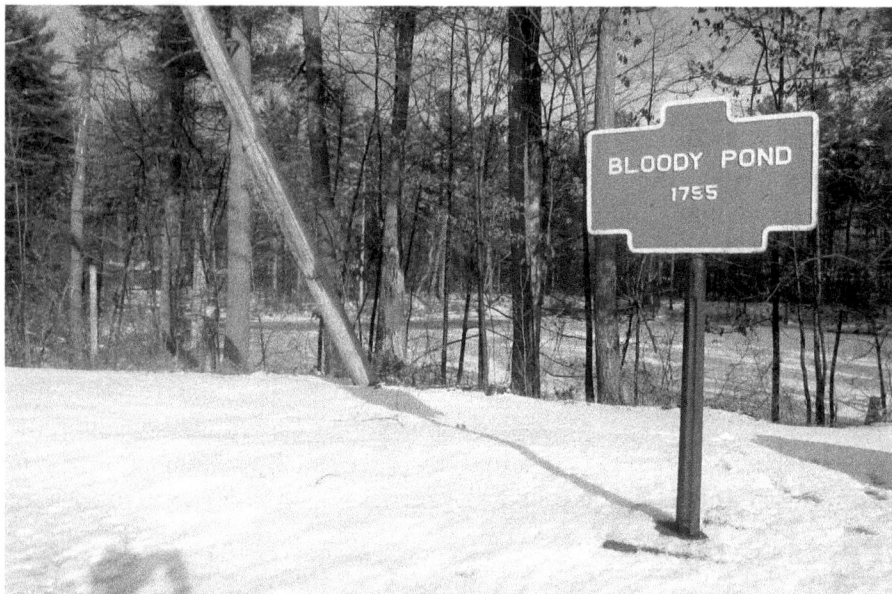

Bloody Pond. Note: It is possible that this pond was man-made and that the original site of the now dried pond is actually farther back in the woods. *Author's collection.*

For the time being, the New Hampshire men and New Yorkers needed time to regroup and reorganize before they could continue their advance to the lake. Captain McGinnis was seriously wounded, shot through the head and losing life with every breath he took; six were dead or mortally wounded; and another twenty-one had received injuries. The men made their way through the area that the Canadians and Indians had abandoned, pillaged through their packs and drank fine captured brandy to loosen up their nerves. The enemy was still lurking about in the woods but refused to take back the ground they had lost. The dead from the morning's engagement were still present throughout the woods and along the road. Many of them had been stripped of their clothing and scalped. Others were seen tied to trees with their bodies mutilated. It was a harrowing sight to behold, portraying to the men firsthand the horrors of the war that was being waged.[130]

Around sunset the New Yorkers began to file into the road to head back to the safe confines of Fort Lyman. Captain Folsom frustratingly inquired where the men were going and warned them that if they left they would "sacrifice their own lives & ours too." "They would not stay there to be killed by the damn'd Indians after dark," they shot back, "but would go off by daylight." So there the detachment remained for the rest of the night. "Between sunset and the shutting in of daylight we call'd to our enemies," Folsom recounted. "[We] told them we had a thousand come to our assistance; that we should have them immediately in our hands." The provincial companies shouted and beat their drums to simulate the sound of a much larger force, and eventually the enemy made their retreat. It is not clear exactly when Folsom and his men arrived at the camp with their wounded. He claimed that they departed from the battlefield and headed north at daylight, but then he later contradicted that statement, saying that they arrived after midnight. Regardless, his men marched triumphantly into the encampment, and "the whole army shouted for joy" at the news of the road being cleared of all enemies. The victory was complete, but not at a low cost.[131]

The Battle of Lake George had been fought in three separate phases that spanned at least eight hours. When the smoke cleared and the casualty reports were made, both sides could count a combined 670 men dead, wounded, captured or missing. Johnson's army counted 154 dead, 103 wounded and 67 missing, many of who were later found dead. The majority of the casualties came from the Third Massachusetts Regiment, which suffered a recorded 70 men dead, wounded or missing—nearly all from the morning's fight. The Mohawks had lost 60 warriors in the engagement, including their beloved Hendrick. The number of French losses is fairly consistent. The official journal of operations listed the casualty count at 149 dead, 163 wounded and 27 taken prisoners. Many of those dead and wounded were a result of the fighting at Bloody Pond. For the days following the battle, the somber work of burying the dead was conducted. Men like John Burk participated as a member of the burial detail, and he noted that along with laying the dead to rest, the men also "Brought in a great deal of plunder and French provisions." This was the reward for completing such an unenviable series of tasks.[132]

William Johnson's army lost eighteen commissioned officers during the fighting on September 8, including Colonels Titcomb and Williams. Captains Hawley and McGinnis lingered from their wounds in the days to come, but both eventually succumbed. William Johnson survived his wound but never chose to have the ball removed; it would ail him for the remainder of his life. He was confined to his tent while writing his official report to the royal governors on September 9. In his report, not once did he mention Phineas Lyman or Nathan Whiting, to whose leadership he owed the victory. For months following the battle a controversy would rage between the three men, manifesting into a regional rivalry for the legacy of the engagement between Connecticut and New York. Things became so bitter that before the year was over, Johnson changed the name of Fort Lyman to Fort Edward.[133]

As September dragged on, no effort was made to continue the campaign against Crown Point. Despite the repeated pushes from William Shirley to attack, Johnson was adamant that he had neither the manpower nor the resources necessary to undertake another expedition before the summer was over. His Mohawk allies were leaving camp and returning home, and so, too, were a handful of the provincials, reducing the size of his army by the hundreds. The chief concern for the commanding general was erecting a larger permanent fortification at the base of the lake to deter the French from using it as an avenue of invasion into New York's interior. After several scouts by Robert Rogers and his company of rangers, it was discovered that the French had begun their own construction of a massive stone fortress, later to be name Fort Carillon (Ticonderoga). This was evidence that the French intended to hold the northern end of Lake George and launch future raids south. By September 29, Johnson and Eyre finally planned the construction of a large wooden Vauban-style fortification (square with four protruding bastions on each corner) a little to the west of the battlefield on high ground overlooking the lake. On November 13, 1755, the gates were open, and the newly christened Fort William Henry was garrisoned.[134]

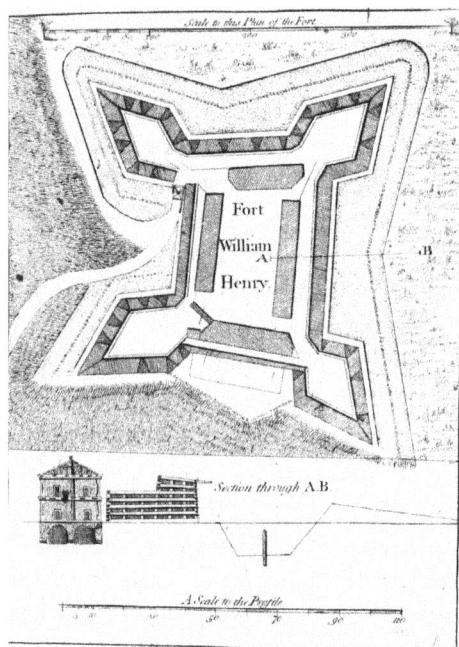

Fort William Henry. *From* A Set of Plans and Forts in North America *(1765)*.

Jean-Armand, Baron de Dieskau, survived his wounds as well and was transferred to New York City and then to London, where he remained until the Treaty of Paris was signed in 1763. He returned home and never held another battlefield command. He died in 1767. In May 1756, Dieskau's replacement, forty-four-year-old Louis-Joseph, Marquis de Montcalm, arrived in Quebec and assumed command of all French Regulars in North America. That same month, war was officially declared in

Europe, and the world was set ablaze. Montcalm acted swiftly and for three years presented Louis XV nothing but victories in North America, capturing Forts Bull and Oswego in 1756 and Fort William Henry in 1757. He then defeated a massive British army under James Abercromby outside Fort Carillon on July 8, 1758. England did not fully claim all of Lake George until the following year, when the French retreated from Ticonderoga and the war moved north into Canada, where in September an army under the command of James Wolfe mauled Montcalm's forces on the Plains of Abraham outside Quebec. Both generals were mortally wounded in the fighting and later succumbed

Louis Joseph, Marquis de Montcalm. *Courtesy of New York Public Library Digital Collections.*

to their injuries. Quebec's capitulation triggered a domino effect that led to the fall of Montreal in 1760 and, with it, France's territorial claim in North America. In February 1763, the Treaty of Paris was signed, officially ending the Seven Years' War.[135]

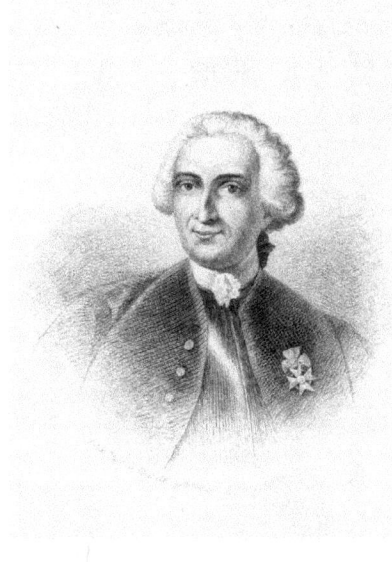

One hundred years passed before the first monument dedicated to the Battle of Lake George was unveiled. In 1854, alumni of Williams College in Williamstown, Massachusetts, erected a marble obelisk atop the boulder believed to be the spot where Ephraim Williams was killed during the Bloody Morning Scout. In July 1755, Williams, as part of his last will and testament, specified that his land not being distributed to family members be "appropriated toward the support and maintenance of a free school." That land became Williams College in 1793, and Ephraim's memory was honored with the obelisk and the town that bears his name today. A day following the battle, members of the Third Massachusetts returned to the site of Williams's death, recovered the body of their colonel and buried it on high ground overlooking the military road. The body was exhumed in the 1830s by a relative and brought to North Carolina. In 1920, the remains were taken back home to Massachusetts, where they now permanently rest in the Williamstown Thompson Memorial Chapel.[136]

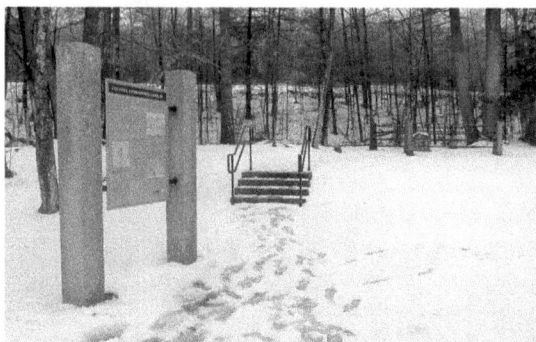

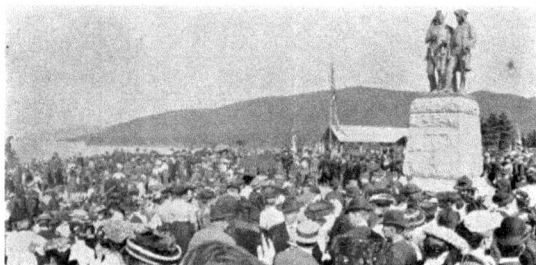

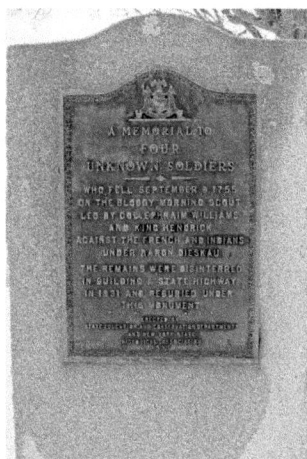

Above: Detail view of the final resting place of four men killed during the Bloody Morning Scout, Lake George Battlefield Park. *Author's collection.*

Top: Modern-day view of the site of Ephraim Williams's original burial place near the Bloody Morning Scout battlefield. *Author's collection.*

Bottom: The dedication and unveiling of the Lake George Battle Monument, September 8, 1903. *Author's collection.*

Another fifty years went by when, finally, the Society of Colonial Wars in the State of New York unveiled a statue of William Johnson and his friend King Hendrick on September 8, 1903. The monument stands as a memorial to the provincial and Indian victory in 1755 and now serves as the centerpiece of the Lake George Battlefield Park. A handful of other monuments have been erected within the confines of the park since then to commemorate the fighting. Not far from the Battle Monument, the remains of four men killed during the Bloody Morning Scout, uncovered in 1931 during highway construction, are buried in a small grave beneath a stone memorial and tablet. Roughly a stone's throw away from this position is a beautiful statue of a Native American dipping his hand in a pool of water. The monument is dedicated to all indigenous people of the Adirondacks and is a poignant reminder that without the Indians' help, the English could never have prospered in North America.

Any trip today to the Lake George area warrants a visit to the site of the 1755 battle. In the summer months the southern shore of the lake is

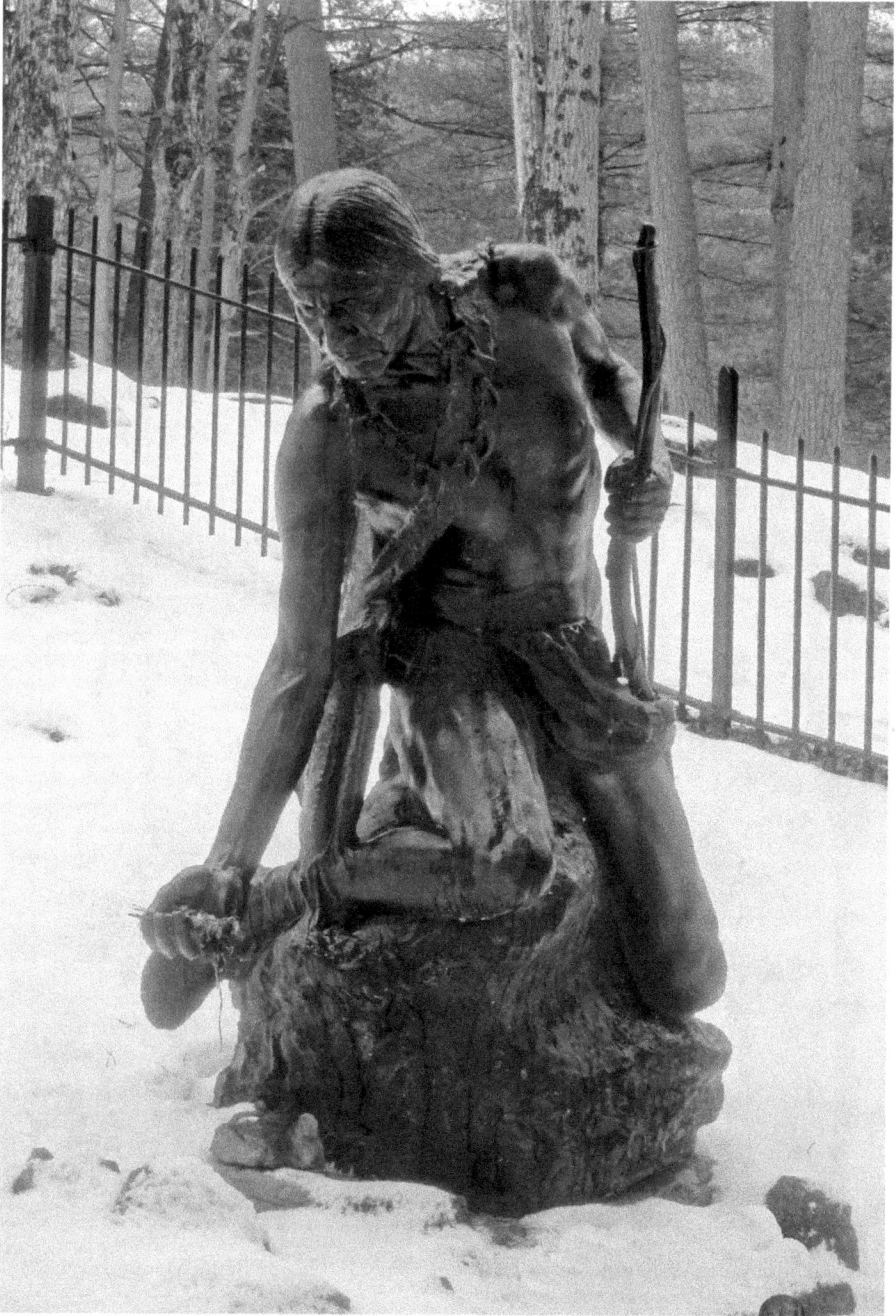

The Indian, monument to Native Americans, Lake George Battlefield Park. *Author's collection.*

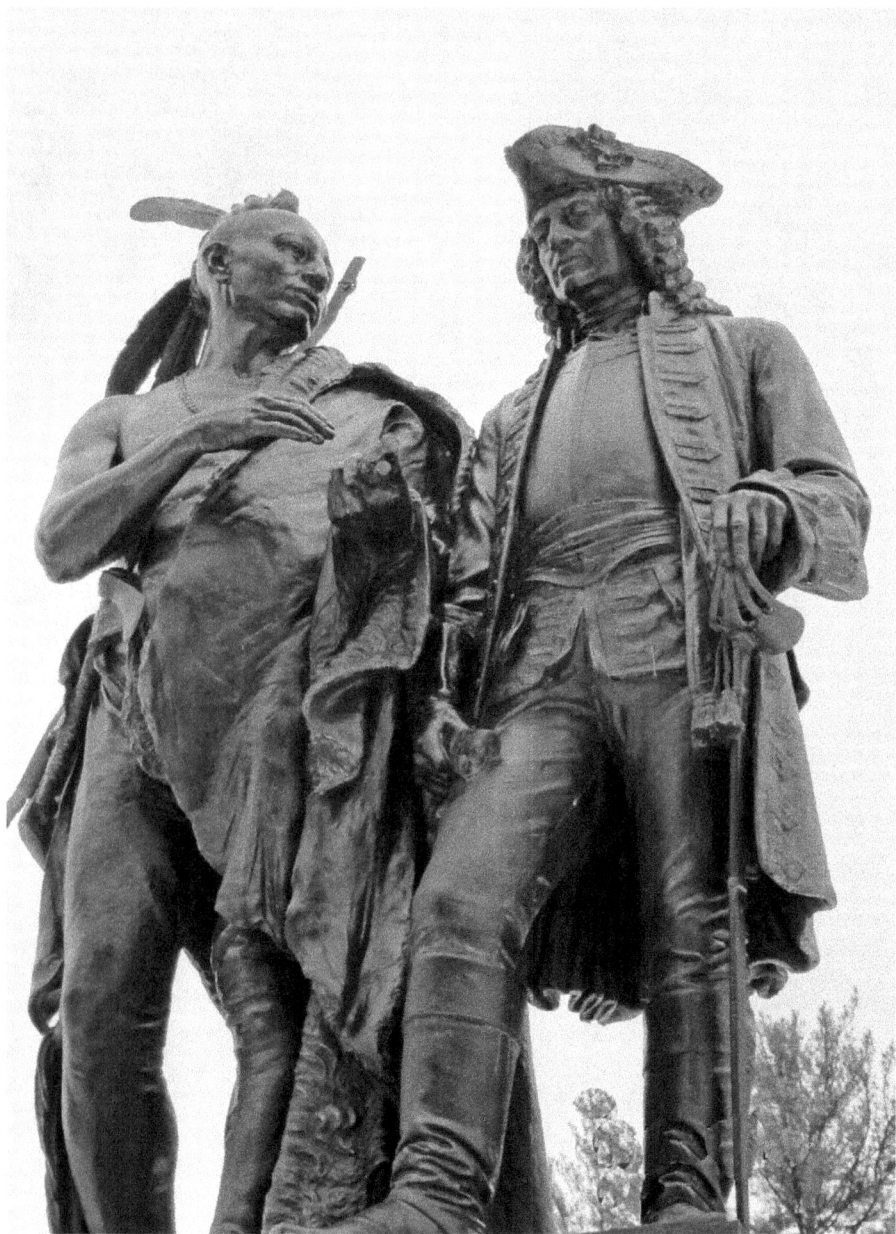

King Hendrick and William Johnson stand atop the Lake George Battle Monument, Lake George Battlefield Park. *Author's collection.*

crawling with tourist activity, and it is extremely difficult to believe that one could be standing on what was perhaps one of the most important and widely disputed pieces of ground in all of North America. Despite this fact, it is crucial to understand that what is today a destination for family fun and summer recreation, over 260 years ago was the site of what surgeon Thomas Williams sorrowfully described as "the most awful day that my eyes ever beheld."[137]

9

CONCLUSION

*T*he Battle of Lake George was a clear-cut victory for William Johnson's army in every sense. Tactically, his men drove the French from the battlefield and sent them fleeing north to Carillon. Strategically, although Johnson did not capture his main objective—Fort St. Frédéric—he was able to defend Upstate New York, secure the southern shore of Lake George for future operations and put an end to France's offensive against England in that sector as well. Not to mention, following Braddock's defeat it was imperative that England's military forces in North America counter with a victory of their own, which they did on September 8, 1755. Morale in the British colonies heightened, while in New France, according to one Canadian soldier, "The news of the French defeat in this engagement caused gloom in Canada, where they had much faith in the help sent them from France."[138]

Since the nineteenth century, historians have been belittling the success of the provincials at the battle of Lake George because they only analyze what Johnson did afterward. A military victory is not measured by what transpires after a battle. Because Johnson abandoned his campaign against Crown Point does not mean that the victory at Lake George was a hollow one. Following the Confederate victory at the Battle of Chancellorsville in May 1863, Robert E. Lee turned his attention to the north and invaded Maryland and Pennsylvania the following month. As history tells us, his Army of Northern Virginia was defeated by the Army of the Potomac outside Gettysburg on July 1–3, and Lee was forced to take his rebels south to Virginia with nothing more to show than twenty-three thousand men lost who could not be replaced. Yet today Chancellorsville is heralded as one of the greatest military achievements in American history. Chancellorsville is its own entity and does not get belittled at all when it is associated with the Gettysburg campaign. The Battle of Lake George should be studied objectively as its own event within the larger context of a terrible year for the British military in North America, not as a footnote in a "failed" campaign.

"The Crown Point expedition," in the words of Francis Parkman, "was a failure disguised under an incidental success." The word *incidental* is entirely inaccurate, implying that the battle was unplanned; this is not at all the case. Johnson was well aware that Dieskau was at least at Crown Point with a large force, and by September 7 he knew that the French had landed at South Bay and were advancing south, most likely to attack Fort Lyman. If Johnson was not expecting a battle with the French, he would have never dispatched a third of his entire army to support Blanchard at the Great Carrying Place. Historian Ian K. Steele agreed that the provincials had won a battle by "European standards" but argued that the men were demoralized and did not receive any sort of boost in confidence. What needs to be taken into account is that nearly every man fighting that day—besides the older veterans of King George's War—had never witnessed any form of combat in their lives. They were not professional soldiers and just played a part in the second-bloodiest battle ever fought in the English colonies. The mental effect on the men must have been great, and to their credit, they beat back repeated attacks by some of the best regular troops that France could supply in North America.[139]

In his 2005 study *Empires at War*, William M. Fowler labeled Robert Monckton's capture of the French forts in Nova Scotia as the only "exception" in a terrible year of war for England in North America. The conquest of the Chignecto Isthmus was definitely a bright spot in 1755, but there is no reason that Lake George should not be included as part of that. Between July and August William Johnson's army had built a road seventy miles long and held and secured it after it was put under the threat of an enemy force. That path served as one of the most important military road networks in the colonies throughout the duration of the war. While Crown Point still remained in French hands, so, too, did the southern shore of Lake George and the main artery leading down to Albany remain in England's. If Johnson's army had been defeated, the way into New York's interior would have been wide open to the French and the water highway system from Quebec would have been lost. Although the entirety of the lake was not captured by the

British until 1759, the victory on its southern shore in 1755 prevented a disaster probably even greater in consequence than Braddock's defeat.[140]

In the end, it is important to understand that the Battle of Lake George must also be viewed from France's perspective rather than just England's. Dieskau's orders were to reinforce Crown Point and defeat Johnson's army and send it scurrying from the lake to prevent any further threats against their possessions in New York—which he failed to achieve. While Crown Point remained firmly in French hands, the British gained a base of operations to use for the next four years. The southern shore became home to thousands of British Regulars and provincials who would eventually make their way north to Canada. For years the battle has remained a footnote in colonial history despite the fact that it was England's first major battlefield victory against the French in North America. The men who fought in the engagement never forgot the sacrifices made that day, the family and friends lost and the sights and sounds that were to forever be etched into their memories. The memory and legacy of the Battle of Lake George can best be described by one of its key participants, Phineas Lyman, who wrote to his wife after the fighting, "Praise and Bless [God's] name and forever remember the 8th of September." We owe it to those men to never forget.[141]

BATTLE REPORTS OF THE COMMANDING GENERALS AT LAKE GEORGE

WILLIAM JOHNSON'S REPORT TO THE GOVERNORS

Camp at Lake George 9th. September. 1755

Sir,

Sunday evening the 7th. Inst. I received Intelligence from some Indian Scouts, I had sent out, that they had discovered Three large roads about the South Bay, and were Confident a very Considerable Number of the Enemy were Marched or on their March Toowards our Encampment at the Carrying Place, where were Posted about 250 of the New Hampshire Troops, and five Companies of the New York Regiment: I got One Adams a Waggoner, who Voluntarily and Bravely Consented to Ride Express with my Orders to Colonel Blanchard of the New Hampshire Regiment, Commanding Officer there; I Acquainted him with my Intelligence, and directed him to withdraw all the Troops there within the Works thrown up. About half an hour, or near an hour after this, I got Two Indians and Two Soldiers to go on foot with Another Letter to the Same Purpose.

About 12 O'Clock that night the Indians And Soldiers returned with a Waggoner who had Stole from the Camp with about 8 others their Waggons and horses without orders from this side the Carrying Place; they heard a Gun fire, and a man call upon Heaven for Mercy, which he judged to be Adams; the next morning I called a Council of War, who gave it as their opinion, and in which the Indians were Extremely Urgent, That 1000 men should be detached and a Number of their People would go with them in order to Catch the Enemy in their Retreat from the other Camp, either as Victors or defeated in their Designs. The 1000 men were detached under the Command of Colonel Williams of one of the Boston Regiments with Upwards of 200 Indians. They Marched between 8 & 9 O'Clock in about an Hour And a half afterwards we heard a heavy firing, and all the Marks of a Warm Engagement, which we Judged was about 3 or 4 Miles from us: We beat to Arms, and got our men all in readiness; the fire Approached nearer, upon which I judged our People were Retreating and Detached Lieutenant Colonel Cole with about 300 men to Cover their Retreat: About 10 O'Clock some of our men in the rear, and some Indians of Said Party came running into Camp, And Acquainted us that our men were retreating, that the Enemy were to Strong for them; The Whole Party that escaped returned to us in large Bodies. As we had thrown up a Breast Work of Trees round our Encampment, and Planted Field Pieces to defend the Same, We Immediately hawled Some heavy Cannon up there to Strengthen our Front, Took possession of some Eminences on our left Flank and got one field piece there in a very Advantageous Situation; the Breast work was manned throughout by our People, and the best Disposition made thro' our whole Encampment which time and Circumstances would permit; about half an hour after 11 the Enemy appeared in Sight, And Marched along the road in very regular order, directly upon our Center; they made a Small halt about 150 Yards from our breast work, when the Regular Troops (whom we Judged to be such by their bright and fix't Bayonets) made the Grand and Center Attack; The Canadians and Indians Squatted, and Dispersed on our Flanks; The Enemy's fire we received first from their regulars in Platoons, but it did no great Execution being at too great a Distance, and our men defended by the Breast Work; Our Artillery then began to Play on them, and was Served Under the direction of Capt. Eyre during the Whole Engagement in a manner very Advantageous to his Character, And those Concerned in the Management of it: The Engagement now became General on both Sides: The French regulars kept their ground and Order for Some time with great resolution and good Conduct; but the Warm and Constant fire from our Artillery and Troops Put them into Disorder — their fire became more Scattered and Unequal; and the Enemy's fire on our Left grew very faint; they moved then to the right of Our Encampment , and Attacked Col. Ruggles, Col. Williams and Col. Titcomb's Regiments, where they Maintained a very Warm fire for near an hour, Still keeping up their fire in the other Parts of our Line, tho not very Strong. The three regiments on the Right Supported the

Attack very resolutely, and kept a Constant and Strong fire upon the Enemy: This Attack failing, and the Artillery Still Playing along the line, we found their fire very weak, with Several Intervals. This was about 4 O'Clock, when our men and the Indians Jump'd over the breast Work, Pursued the Enemy, Slaughtered numbers, and took Several Prisoners, Amongst whom is the Baron De Dieskau, the French General of all the Regular forces lately Arrived from Europe, who was brought to my Tent about 6 O'Clock, Just as a Wound I had received was Dressed; The Whole Engagement and Pursuit ended about Seven O'Clock – I don't know whether I can get the returns of the Slain and Wounded on our Side to transmit herewith, but more of that by And by; The greatest loss, we have Sustained, was in the Party Commanded by Col. Williams in the morning, who was Attacked And the men gave way before Col. Whiting, who brought up the rear, Cou'd come to his Assistance; The Enemy, who were more Numerous, Endeavoured to Surround them; Upon which the Officers found they had no way to Save the Troops, but by retreating; which they did as fast as they Could: In this Engagement we Suffered Our greatest Loss; Col. Williams, Major Ashely, Capt. Ingersol and Capt. Puter of the Same Regiment, Capt. Farrell, a Brother in Law to the General, who Commanded a Party of Indians, Capt. Stoddart, Capt. Magin, Capt. Stevens, all Indian Officers, and, the Indians Say, near 40 of their People, who fought like Lyons, were all Slain. Old Hendrick, the great Mohawk Sachem, we fear is kill'd.

We have abundant reason to think we killed a great Number of the Enemy, Amongst whom is Monsieur St. Pierre, who Comanded All the Indians; the Exact number on either Side I cannot Obtain; for tho': I sent a Party to Bury our Dead this afternoon, it being a running Scattered Engagement we can neither find all our dead nor give an Exact Account; As fast as these Troops Joined us, they formed with the rest in the Main Battle of the Day, so that the Killed and Wounded in both Engagements, Officers Excepted, must Stand upon One return.

About 8 O'Clock last night a Party of 120 of the New Hampshire Regiment, and 90 of the New York Regiment, who were Detached to our Assistance under the Command of Capt. Maginnes [McGinnis] *from the Camp at the Carrying Place to reinforce us, were Attacked by a Party of Indians and Canadians at the Place where Colonel Williams was Attacked in the morning; their Engagement began between 4 & 5 O'Clock; this Party, who, our People say, were between 3 & 400, had fled from the Engagement here, and gone to Scalp our People killed in the Morning; Our Brave men fought them for near 2 Hours, and made a Considerable*

Slaughter amongst them; of this Party 2 are Killed, 11 Wounded, and 5 Missing; Captain [McGinnis], who behaved with the Utmost Calmness & Resolution, was brought on a Horse here, and I fear his Wounds will Prove Mortal; Ensign Falsam, of the New Hampshire Regiment, Wounded thro the Shoulder.

I this Morning Called a Council of War, a Copy of the Minutes of which I send you herewith.

Monsieur Le Baron De Dieskau, the French General is badly Wounded in the Leg and thro' both his Hipps, and the Surgeon very much fears his Life; He is an Elderly Gentlemen, an Experienced Officer, and a man of high Consideration in France; from his Papers I find he brought under his Command to Canada in the men of War lately Arrived at [Quebec] 3171 Regular Troops, who are partly in Garrison at Crown Point, and Encamped at Ticonderoga, and other Advantageous Passes between this and Crown Point; he tells me he had with him Yesterday morning – 200 Grenadiers, 800 Canadians, and 700 Indians of Different Nations. His Aid De Camp Says (they being Separately Asked) their Whole Force was about 2000; Several of the Prisoners say about 2300 – The Baron Says his Major General was killed, And his Aid De Camp Says the greatest Part of their Chief Officers; also he thinks by the Morning and afternoon Actions they have lost near 1000 men, but I can get no regular Accounts; most of our people think from [4] to 500. We have about 30 Prisoners most of them badly Wounded; The Indians Scalped of their Dead already near 70 – And Were Employed after, the last night, and all this Morning, in bringing in Scalps; and great numbers of French & Indians yet left Unscalped; they Carried off numbers of their Dead and Secreted them: Our men have suffered so much Fatigue for 3 Days Past, and are Constantly Standing upon their Arms by Day, half the Whole upon Guard every Night, and the rest Lay down Armed and Accoutered, both Officers and men Are Almost wore out; The Enemy may rally, and we Judge they have Considerable reinforcements near at Hand, so that I think it Necessary we be upon our Guard, and be Watchfull to Maintain the Advantage, we have gained; for these reasons Don't think it Either prudent or Safe to be sending out parties in Search of the Dead.

I don't hear of any Officer kill'd at our Camp, but Col. Titcomb, and none wounded but myself and Major Nicoles of Col. Titcomb's; I cannot yet get a Certain return of our dead And wounded; but from the best Accounts, I can Obtain, we have lost about 130 who are Kill'd, about 60 Wounded, & Several Missing from the morning and Afternoon's Engagements.

I think we may Expect very Shortly another, and More Formidable Attack, And that the Enemy will then Come With Artillery; The late Col. Williams had the Ground Cleared for Building a Stockaded Fort; our men so harras'd, And Obliged to be so Constantly on Watchfull Duty, That I think it wou'd be both Unreasonable, and, I fear in Vain, to Set them at Work upon the Design'd Fort.

I Design to order the New Hampshire Regiment up here to reinforce Us, and I hope some of the Designed reinforcements will be with us in a few Days, When those fresh Troops Arrive I Shall Immediately set About Building a Fort –

My Wound which is in my Thigh is very Painfull, the Ball is lodg'd and Cannot be got out by which means I am to my Mortification Confined to my Tent.

10ʰ. This letter was begun and Should have been Dispatched Yesterday, but we have had Two Alarms and Neither time nor Prudence would permit it. I hope Your Excellency will Place the Incorrectness hereof to the Account of our Situation.

I am Most respectfully &c.
William Johnson[142]

BARON DE DIESKAU'S REPORT ON THE CAMPAIGN

Camp of the English army at Lake St. Sacrament,
14ʰ [September], 1755.

My Lord [Count d'Argenson],

I have had the honor to report to you everything of interest to the service, up to my departure for Fort St. Frédéric.

On the very vague intelligence of the designs of the English in that quarter, I proceeded thither with 3000 men, whereof 700 were Regulars, 1600 Canadians and 700 Indians. I arrived at Fort St. Frédéric on the 16ʰ and 17ʰ of August; a portion of the troops had preceded me; the remainder joined me there without delay.

Before quitting Montreal, I had already various reasons for suspecting the fidelity of the domiciliated Iroquois, both of the Sault St. Louis and of the

Lake of the Two Mountains, whose number exceeded 300, composing half of the Indians that had been given to me. I represented it repeatedly to M. de Vaudreuil, who would never admit it, but scarcely had I arrived at Fort St. Frédéric, than I had occasion to furnish him still stronger proofs thereof.

For more than 15 days that I was encamped under that fort, I encountered nothing but difficulties from the Indians; those who were good, were spoiled by the Iroquois. Never was I able to obtain from them a faithful scout; at one time they refused to make any; at another time, seeming to obey me, they set forth, but when a few leagues from the camp, they sent back the Frenchman I had associated with them, and used to return within a few days without bringing me any intelligence. Such has been the conduct of the Indians, caused by the Iroquois. My letters from Fort St. Frédéric to M. de Vaudreuil and M. Bigot, sufficiently develop the particulars of their mischievous intrigues.

At length, on the 27th of August, a Canadian named Boileau, returned from a scout and informed me that about 3000 English were encamped at [Lydius's] house, where they were constructing a fort that was already pretty well advanced. I immediately resolved to go forward and to post myself in an advantageous place, either to wait for the enemy, should he advance, or to anticipate him myself, by going in quest of him.

On arriving at this point [Ticonderoga], some Abenakis who had been on the scout, unknown to the Iroquois, brought me in an English prisoner, who told me that the body of the English army had moved from [Lydius's], and that only 500 remained there to finish the fort, but that they were expecting 2400 men, who were to march to the head of Lake St. Sacrament for the purpose of building a fort there also.

On this intelligence I determined to leave the main body of the army where I was, and to take with me a picked force (corps d'élite) march rapidly and surprise Fort [Lydius], and capture the 500 men encamped within its walls. My detachment was composed of 600 Indians, 600 Canadians and 200 Regulars belonging to La Reine and Languedoc regiments. It was four days' journey by water and across the woods to [Lydius's]. All exhibited an ardor which guaranteed success, but the fourth day, which ought to be favorable to the King's arms, was the commencement of our misfortune.

The Iroquois refused point blank to march to attack the fort, or rather the camp of the 500 English; but, perceiving that I was resolved to dispense with them, and that the other Indians were disposed to follow me, they sent excuses and immediately set forth to lead the van, as if to make a parade of their zeal.

Mine was a combined movement. I was to arrive at nightfall at the fort and rush to the attack; but the Iroquois, who took lead on the march, under the pretense of zeal, caused a wrong direction to be taken; and when I was informed of the circumstances, it was no longer time to apply a remedy, so that at nightfall I was yet a league from that fort on the road leading from it to Lake St. Sacrament.

A courier that was killed, and whose dispatch was brought to me, and some prisoners that were brought in, gave me the intelligence that about 3000 English were encamped near there, and that they had but a confused knowledge of the strength of my forces. I immediately gave the Indians the choice of proceeding next day to attack either the fort or this army. The vote of the Iroquois which prevailed caused the latter course to be adopted.

On the following day, the 8th of September, I commenced my march. About 10 of the clock, after having proceeded 5 leagues, the scouts reported to me that they had seen a large body of troops on their way to the fort, which news was confirmed by a prisoner, taken at the time. They consisted of one thousand men or more, that had left the camp to reinforce the fort. I immediately made my arrangements, ordered the Indians to throw themselves into the woods, to allow the enemy to pass, so as to attack them in the rear, whilst the Canadians took them on the flank, and I should wait for them in front with the regular troops.

This was the moment of treachery. The Iroquois, who were on the left, showed themselves before the time and did not fire. The Abenakis, who occupied the right, seeing themselves discovered, alone with a few Canadians attacked the enemy in front and put them to flight. I immediately prepared to join them, in order to accompany the fugitives into their camp, though still more than a league off.

Meanwhile, the Iroquois collected on a hill, unwilling to advance. Some of them even wanted to force the Abenakis to release three Mohawks whom they had captured at the first encounter. I am ignorant of the result of that quarrel; but the Abenakis, seeing the Iroquois immovable, halted also, and the Canadians, seeing the retreat of the one and the other, were thereby intimidated.

As I was near the enemy's camp, and in front of the cannon, I marched forward with 200 Regulars to capture it, [expecting] *that the Canadians would not abandon me, and that the Indians would perhaps return; but in vain. The Regulars received the whole of the enemy's fire and perished there almost to a man. I was knocked down by three shots, none of which were mortal, but I received a 4th that passed from one hip to the other, perforating the bladder.*

I know not at present what will be my fate; from M. de Johnson, the General of the English army, I am receiving all the attention possible to be expected from a brave man, full of honor and feeling. Sieur de Bernier, my Aid de Camp, is a prisoner with me; he has been fortunate enough to receive only a slight bruise from a splinter. I know not of any other officers taken.

Should the nature of my wounds destroy the hope of returning to Europe, and should Sieur Bernier go there, he will be able to give you, my Lord, the fullest detail of this affair, and of everything that my situation prevents me explaining to you.

I beg of you, my Lord, to have regard for his zeal for the service, and for his attachment to me.

> *I have the honor to be respectfully, My Lord,*
> *Your most humble and most obedient servant,*
> *Baron de Dieskau*[143]

THE CAMPAIGNS OF 1755

A CHRONOLOGY

1748
October 18—Treaty of Aix-la-Chapelle is signed, ending the War of Austrian Succession (King George's War in North America).

1753
December 11—George Washington arrives at Fort Le Boeuf and meets with Captain Jacques Legardeur de St. Pierre with orders from Royal Governor Dinwiddie for the French to evacuate the Ohio River Valley. He returns to Virginia three days later.

1754
April 16—French forces seize the Forks of the Ohio River and begin construction of Fort Duquesne.

May 28—George Washington leads a small detachment of Virginians and Mingo warriors against a party of French-Canadians commanded by Ensign Joseph Coulon de Villiers de Jumonville.

June 19—Delegates from seven of the thirteen colonies and Iroquois representatives meet in Albany, New York, to address Native American grievances and devise a plan of unification against the French. The Congress is disbanded in July.

July 3–4—The Battle of Fort Necessity. George Washington, in command of four hundred Virginians and South Carolinians, is attacked by a force of Canadians and Native Americans at Great Meadows. His men surrender to Ensign Jumonville's older brother, and Washington unknowingly signs a document confessing to the murder of the French "diplomat" on May 28.

September 15—Major General Edward Braddock is appointed commander in chief of His Majesty's Forces in North America.

December 22—Braddock and his military family, onboard the HMS *Norwich*, embark for Virginia.

1755
February 19—Braddock arrives at Hampton Roads, Virginia.

March 1—Jean-Armand, Baron de Dieskau, is appointed *maréchal de camp* of French regular troops being sent to New France.

March 10—The Forty-fourth and Forty-eighth Regiments of Foot arrive in Virginia.

April 1—Pierre Francois, Marquis de Vaudreuil de Cavagnal, is appointed governor-general of New France.

April 14–15—Braddock, William Johnson and the royal governors of Maryland, Massachusetts, New York, Pennsylvania and Virginia meet at the home of John Carlyle in Alexandria, Virginia, to discuss the upcoming campaigns against the French in New York, Nova Scotia and Pennsylvania. Johnson is appointed to the position of superintendent of Indian affairs in the Northern Colonies.

May 3—Dieskau, Vaudreuil and over three thousand French Regulars embark on their journey across the Atlantic to Louisbourg and Quebec.

May 5—Braddock and Washington arrive at Winchester, Virginia, and proceed to Fort Cumberland.

May 26—Massachusetts militiamen disembark from Boston and sail to Annapolis Royal on the Bay of Fundy. Once there, they rendezvous with Robert Monckton and his regulars.

May 29—Braddock's army departs from Fort Cumberland and begins its march to the Forks of the Ohio River.

June 9—Admiral Edward Boscawen captures two straggling ships carrying three hundred French Regulars destined for North America.

June 13—The siege of Fort Beauséjour commences.

June 16—Fort Beauséjour surrenders to Robert Monckton.

June 18—Fort Gaspereau surrenders to Monckton without firing a shot.

June 21—Over one thousand Iroquois men, women and children gather at Mount Johnson.

June 23—Dieskau and Vaudreuil arrive in Quebec.

June 30—Phineas Lyman arrives in Albany.

July 7—William Johnson arrives in Albany.

July 9—The Battle of the Monongahela. Braddock and his force of over thirteen hundred men engage the French only miles away from Fort Duquense. Suffering over nine hundred casualties (Braddock among them), the British and provincial force flee the battlefield and begin their long journey to Philadelphia in full retreat.

July 10—William Shirley arrives in Albany.

July 13—Edward Braddock succumbs to his wounds received four days prior and is buried in the middle of his road the next day. William Shirley is now commander in chief.

July 14—Johnson and Shirley hold a grand review of the regiments mustered near Albany.

July 17—What is left of Braddock's army begins to arrive at Fort Cumberland; Phineas Lyman is ordered forward with a contingent of Johnson's army to the Great Carrying Place, where he is to begin constructing Fort Lyman (Edward).

July 22—Lyman takes the First Connecticut and Second and Third Massachusetts Regiments with him to the Great Carrying Place, widening the road from Albany along the way.

July 24—Lyman and his wing arrive at Stillwater and encamp for four days to clear and widen the military road north of Albany.

July 29—Lyman and his wing arrive at Saratoga.

August 3—Lyman and his wing arrive at the Great Carrying Place and begin constructing Fort Lyman.

August 6—Moses Titcomb departs from above Albany with the second division (Second Massachusetts, Second Connecticut and the remaining companies of the Third Massachusetts) and begins marching his column to Fort Lyman.

August 11—Colonel Joseph Blanchard's First New Hampshire Regiment arrives at Albany.

August 12—Vaudreuil orders Dieskau to call off his advance to Lake Ontario and instead move to Fort St. Frédéric to oppose Johnson's force; Lyman sends forward a working party of three hundred men to clear and widen the military road from Fort Lyman to Wood Creek.

August 14—Johnson arrives at Fort Lyman (Great Carrying Place).

August 15—Titcomb's division arrives at Fort Lyman.

August 16—Dieskau arrives at Fort St. Frédéric with his force of three thousand men. The garrison at Crown Point is roughly five hundred strong before that.

August 17—William Shirley and the majority of his force arrive at Fort Oswego; the First Rhode Island and First New York Regiments arrive at Fort Lyman.

August 20—Dieskau's army of 3,573 men arrives at Crown Point.

August 26—Johnson departs Fort Lyman with fifteen hundred men and advances toward Lake George.

August 28—Johnson arrives at the southern end of Lake George.

August 30—King Hendrick and roughly 160 Mohawk warriors arrive at Johnson's camp.

September 2—Dieskau moves his army to the prominence of Ticonderoga, future site of Fort Carillon; the remainder of Shirley's expeditionary force arrives at Oswego.

September 3—Lyman and Titcomb arrive at Lake George.

September 4—After interrogating an English prisoner captured by Abenaki scouts outside Fort Lyman, Dieskau advances down Lake Champlain and Wood Creek with fifteen hundred men to assault Fort Lyman; Blanchard's First New Hampshire Regiment arrives at Fort Lyman.

September 5—Dieskau's force reaches the end of South Bay.

September 6—Dieskau's force marches ten miles and encamps.

September 7—Dieskau's force marches twenty miles and encamps several miles away from Fort Lyman. After much debate with his Indian allies about attacking the British position, Dieskau decides to follow Johnson's military road north and assault the provincial encampment at Lake George.

September 8—Battle of Lake George. William Johnson's army of New Englanders, New Yorkers and Mohawk allies defeats Baron de Dieskau's combined force of French regulars, Canadians and Indians at the southern end of Lake George.

September 20—Vaudreuil orders Fort Carillon to be constructed.

September 29—Plans are made to build a permanent fortification at the southern end of Lake George.

November 13—Construction of Fort William Henry is complete.

NOTES

Introduction

1. Ferris, *Account of the Battle of Lake George*, 9.
2. Henry Taylor Blake, *The Battle of Lake George (September 8, 1755) and the Men Who Won It* (Lake George, NY: Read, 1909), 109.

Chapter 1

3. Crocker, *Braddock's March*, 96.
4. Anderson, *The War that Made America*, 61–63.
5. Pargellis, *Military Affairs in North America, 1748–1765*, 81.
6. Ibid., 82.
7. O'Callaghan, *Documents Relative to the Colonial History of the State of New-York*, vol. 6, 116. Hereafter cited as *NYCD*.
8. Ibid.
9. Quoted in Bellico, *Empires in the Mountains*, 44.
10. Pargellis, *Military Affairs in North America*, 81–82.

Chapter 2

11. Sheppard, *Empires Collide*, 21–23.
12. Ibid., 26.

13. Walter Kendall Watkins, "Lake George Expedition 1755," *The Society of Colonial Wars of the Commonwealth of Massachusetts* (Boston: printed for the society), 153–54.

14. Quoted in Pew, *Drums of Ephraim Williams*, 19.

15. Russell, *Guns on the Early Frontiers*, 67.

16. Marston, *The French-Indian War, 1754–1760*, 14.

17. Ibid., 14–16.

18. Berleth, *Bloody Mohawk*, 15; Hugh Hastings, "Sir William Johnson," in New York State Historical Association, *Constitution and By-Laws with Proceedings of the Second Annual Meeting* (New York: New York State Historical Association, 1901), 37.

19. Anderson, *Crucible of War*, 79.

20. Ibid., 91.

21. Bellico, *Empires in the Mountains*, 47.

22. *NYCD*, 993.

23. Clark, *Phineas Lyman*, 3–4; William O. Stearns, "Major-General Phineas Lyman," in New York State Historical Association, *Constitution and By-Laws with Proceedings of the Second Annual Meeting* (New York: New York State Historical Association, 1901), 58–59.

24. Kemmer, *Redcoats, Yankees and Allies*, 61, 63.

25. Connecticut Historical Society, *Rolls of Connecticut Men in the French and Indian War*, 4.

26. Whiting, "Letters of Colonel Nathan Whiting," 133; Blake, "Battle of Lake George," 112–13.

27. Quoted in Blake, "Battle of Lake George," 113.

28. Sullivan, *The Papers of Sir William Johnson*, vol. 1, 553. Hereafter cited as *WJP*.

29. Kemmer, *Redcoats, Yankees and Allies*, 55, 57, 59–60.

30. Watkins, "Lake George Expedition 1755," 177; Stark, 225–26.

31. Lowell, *A Sermon Occasioned by the Much Lamented Death of Col. Moses Titcomb*, 3; *WJP*, 778.

32. James Austin Holden, "Colonel Ephraim Williams," *Constitution and By-Laws with Proceedings of the Second Annual Meeting*, 42–43.

33. Ibid.; Bellico, *Chronicles of Lake George*, 32–33.

34. Pew, *Guns of Ephraim Williams*, 20–24.

35. Bellico, *Empires in the Mountains*, 28–29; Pomeroy, *Journals and Papers of Seth Pomeroy*, 100–1.

36. Farmer, *Catechism of the History of New-Hampshire*, 59; Kemmer, *Redcoats, Yankees and Allies*, 76–77.

37. Kemmer, *Redcoats, Yankees and Allies,* 70–72; Chartrand, *Montcalm's Crushing Blow,* 20.
38. Kemmer, *Redcoats, Yankees and Allies,* 72; Hughes, *The Siege of Fort William Henry,* 138.
39. New York State Historical Society, "Muster Rolls of New York Provincial Troops, 1755–1764," 499, 501; Hollister, *The History of Connecticut,* 508; Roberts, *Genealogies of Connecticut Families,* 521.
40. Roberts, *Genealogies of Connecticut Familes,* 521; Hollister, *History of Connecticut,* 508; "Muster Rolls of New York Provincial Troops," 501; Kemmer, *Redcoats, Yankees and Allies,* 67.
41. McLoughlin, *Rhode Island: A History,* 80–81; Kemmer, *Redcoats, Yankees and Allies,* 73.
42. Bellico, *Empires in the Mountains,* 45–46.
43. Ibid.

Chapter 3

44. Sheppard, *Empires Collide,* 34–35; Bellico, *Empires in the Mountains,* 41.
45. Bellico, *Empires in the Mountains;* Sheppard, *Empires Collide,* 35–36.
46. Halpenny, *Dictionary of Canadian Biography,* 185; Steele, *Betrayals,* 41.
47. Steele, *Betrayals,* 41.
48. *NYCD,* vol. 10, 288–89.
49. Fowler, *Empires at War,* 75–77; Kingsford, *History of Canada,* 522–23.
50. Steele, *Betrayals,* 41; quoted in Fowler, *Empires at War,* 74.
51. Fowler, *Empires at War;* Steele, *Betrayals,* 42–43.
52. Steele, *Betrayals;* Kingsford, *History of Canada,* 524.
53. Sheppard, *Empires Collide,* 100–3.
54. Ibid., 53; *NYCD,* vol. 10, 316.
55. Quoted in Peyser, *Jaques Legardeur de Saint-Pierre,* 225; quoted in Anderson, *Crucible of War,* 44.

Chapter 4

56. *NYCD,* vol. 6, 920.
57. Quoted in Crocker, *Braddock's March,* 103.

58. "General Braddock's Orderly Book, No. 1," in Hadden, *Washington's Early Campaigns*, 151.
59. Ibid., 156–57.
60. Quoted in Anderson, *The War that Made America*, 69.
61. Ibid., 69–71.
62. Anderson, *Crucible of War*, 113.
63. Ibid., 112.
64. Pargellis, *Military Affairs in North America*, 146–47.
65. Quoted in Sheppard, *Empires Collide*, 87.
66. Anderson, *Crucible of War*, 113–14.
67. Chartrand, *Montcalm's Crushing Blow*, 11.
68. Parkman, *Montcalm and Wolfe*, 172–75.

Chapter 5

69. Clark, *Phineas Lyman*, 12–13.
70. Parkman, *Montcalm and Wolfe*, 172; *WJP*, vol. 1, 655.
71. *WJP*, 603.
72. Pomeroy, *Journals and Papers of Seth Pomeroy*, 101–02, 128–29.
73. *WJP*, vol. 1, 730–31.
74. Ibid., 731.
75. Trumball, *History of Northampton*, 255; *Journals and Papers of Seth Pomeroy*, 103.
76. Trumball, *History of Northampton*, 256.
77. *WJP*, vol. 1, 782.
78. Ibid., 777.
79. Pomeroy, *Journals and Papers of Seth Pomeroy*, 104–05; Burk, "John Burk's Diary," in Kellogg, *History of the Town of Bernardston*, 42.
80. *WJP*, vol, 1, 813–16.
81. Whiting, "Letters of Colonel Nathan Whiting," 136–37.
82. *WJP*, vol, 1, 789, 816, 829.
83. Trumball, *History of Northampton*, 256.
84. "John Burk's Diary," 42.
85. Bouton, *Provincial Papers, Documents and Records Relating to the Province of New-Hampshire, from 1749–1763*, vol. 6, 429–30.
86. Quoted in Flexner, *Lord of the Mohawks*, 139; *WJP*, 857.
87. Pomeroy, *Journals and Papers of Seth Pomeroy*, 107–08.
88. Hill, *Old Fort Edward, Before 1800*, 83.

89. Pomeroy, *Journals and Papers of Seth Pomeroy*, 109.
90. Quoted in Clark, *Phineas Lyman*, 16.
91. "John Burk's Diary," 44.
92. *WJP*, vol. 1, 880.
93. Ibid., 880–81.
94. *NYCD*, vol. 10, 316, 319.
95. Quoted in Peyser, *Jacques Legardeur de Saint-Pierre*, 223.
96. *NYCD*, vol. 6, 994.

Chapter 6

97. Ibid., vol. 10, 333–34.
98. Ibid., 335.
99. Ibid., 317.
100. *WJP*, vol. 2, 15–16.
101. Ibid., 17.
102. Claus, *Daniel Claus' Narrative of His Relations with Sir William Johnson*, 12; quoted in Milton W. Hamilton, "Battle Report: General William Johnson's Letter to the Governors, Lake George, September 9–10, 1755," in American Antiquarian Society, *Proceedings of the American Antiquarian Society*, vol. 74 (Worcester, MA: published by the society, 1965), 21.
103. Claus, *Narrative*, 13; Bellico, *Empires in the Mountains*, 58.
104. Trumball, *History of Northampton*, 259.
105. Pew, *Colonel Ephraim Williams*, 15.
106. *NYCD*, vol. 6, 317; Pew, *Colonel Ephraim Williams*, 16.
107. *NYCD*, vol. 6, 331. The Indians allied with France in North America, both economically and militarily, referred to the country as "father," thus why Dieskau uses the term "my children" in his marching orders.
108. Blodget, *A Prospective-Plan of the Battle Near Lake George*, 1.
109. Claus, *Narrative*, 13–14.
110. *NYCD*, vol. 10, 317; Bellico, *Chronicles of Lake George*, 35.
111. Bellico, *Empires in the Mountains*, 61.
112. Pargellis, *Military Affairs*, 139.
113. Pomeroy, *Journals and Papers of Seth Pomeroy*, 114.

Chapter 7

114. Hamilton, "Battle Report: General William Johnson's Letter to the Governors," 22.
115. Pomeroy, *Journals and Papers of Seth Pomeroy*, 114.
116. Wade, *Journals of Francis Parkman*, vol. 2, 570.
117. *NYCD*, vol. 10, 335.
118. Clark, *Phineas Lyman*, 18–19.
119. Pargellis, *Military Affairs*, 139; *NYCD*, vol. 6, 1005.
120. Clark, *Phineas Lyman*, 19.
121. Pargellis, *Military Affairs*, 139; *NYCD*, vol. 10, 317, 335.
122. Hamilton, "Battle Report," 22; Blodget, *Prospective-Plan*, 3.
123. Bellico, *Chronicles of Lake George*, 35–36.
124. *NYCD*, vol. 10, 335.
125. Ibid., vol. 6, 1,005.
126. Hamilton, "Battle Report," 23.

Chapter 8

127. Folsom, "Captain Nathaniel Folsom's Fight," 318.
128. Ibid.
129. Ibid.
130. Ibid.
131. Ibid.
132. *NYCD*, vol. 6, 1,006; Steele, *Betrayals*, 53; "John Burk's Diary," 46.
133. *NYCD*, 1,006.
134. Steele, *Betrayals*, 55.
135. Fowler, *Empires at War*, 95.
136. Bellico, *Empires in the Mountains*, 61.
137. Bellico, *Chronicles of Lake George*, 35.

Chapter 9

138. Gallup, *Memoir of a French and Indian War Soldier*, 121.
139. Parkman, *Montcalm and Wolfe*, 169; Steele, *Betrayals*, 51.
140. Fowler, *Empires at War*, 85.
141. Clarke, *Phineas Lyman*, 19.

Appendix A

142. Hamilton, "Battle Report," 21–24.
143. *NYCD*, vol. 10, 316–18.

BIBLIOGRAPHY

American Antiquarian Society. *Proceedings of the American Antiquarian Society.* Vol. 74. Worcester, MA: published by the society, 1965.

Anderson, Fred. *Crucible of War: The Seven Years' War and the Fate of Empire in British North America, 1754–1766.* New York: Vintage Books, 2000.

———. *A People's Army: Massachusetts Soldiers and Society in the Seven Years' War.* Chapel Hill: University of North Carolina Press, 1984.

———. *The War that Made America: A Short History of the French and Indian War.* New York: Viking Penguin, 2005.

Archives and Special Collections, Williams College. "Ephraim Williams, Jr." http://archives.williams.edu/founding/ewilliams.php.

Bellico, Russell P. *Chronicles of Lake George: Journeys in War and Peace.* Fleishmanns, NY: Purple Mountain Press, 1995.

———. *Empires in the Mountains: French and Indian War Campaigns and Forts in the Lake Champlain, Lake George, and Hudson River Corridor.* Fleishmanns, NY: Purple Mountain Press, 2010.

———. *Bloody Mohawk: The French and Indian War & American Revolution on New York's Frontier.* Hensonville, NY: Black Dome Press Corp., 2009.

Bird, Harrison. *Navies in the Mountains: The Battles on the Waters of Lake Champlain and Lake George, 1609–1814.* New York: Oxford University Press, 1962.

Blake, Henry Taylor. "The Battle of Lake George (September 8, 1755) and the Men Who Won It." *Papers of the New Haven Colony Historical Society.* Vol. 8. New Haven, CT: New Haven Colony Historical Society, 1914.

Blodget, Samuel. *A Prospective-Plan of the Battle Near Lake George on the Eighth Day of September, 1755 with an Explanation Thereof.* Boston, 1756.

Borneman, Walter R. *The French and Indian War: Deciding the Fate of North America.* New York: Harper Perennial, 2006.

Bouton, Nathaniel, ed. *Provincial Papers, Documents and Records Relating to the Province of New-Hampshire, from 1749 to 1763: Containing Very Valuable and Interesting Records and Papers Relating to the Crown Point Expedition, and the "Seven Years French and Indian Wars," 1755–1762.* Manchester, NH: James M. Campbell, State Printer, 1872.

Brumwell, Stephen. *Redcoats: The British Soldier and War in the Americas, 1755–1763.* Cambridge, UK: Cambridge University Press, 2002.

Burk, John. "John Burk's Diary." In *History of the Town of Bernardston,* by Lucy Cutler Kellogg. Greenfield, MA: Press of E.A. Hall & Company, 1902.

Castle, Ian. *Fort William Henry, 1755–57: A Battle, Two Sieges and Bloody Massacre.* New York: Osprey Publishing, 2013.

Chappell, Paul, and Stuart Reid. *King George's Army, 1740–1793: (1) Infantry.* London: Osprey Publishing Ltd., 1995.

Chartrand, Rene. *Montcalm's Crushing Blow: French and Indian Raids Along New York's Oswego River, 1756.* New York: Osprey Publishing, 2014.

Clark, Delphina L.H. *Phineas Lyman: Connecticut's General.* Springfield, MA: Connecticut Valley Historical Museum, 1964.

Claus, Daniel. *Daniel Claus' Narrative of His Relations with Sir William Johnson and Experiences in the Lake George Fight.* New York: Society of Colonial Wars in the State of New York, 1904.

Connecticut Historical Society. *Rolls of Connecticut Men in the French and Indian War, 1755–1762.* Vol. 1. Hartford: Connecticut Historical Society, 1903.

Crocker, Thomas E. *Braddock's March: How the Man Sent to Seize a Continent Changed American History.* Yardley, PA: Westholme Publishing, 2009.

Farmer, John. *Catechism of the History of New-Hampshire, from Its First Settlement to the Present Period.* Concord, NH: Hoag and Atwood, 1830.

Ferris, Morris Patterson. *An Account of the Battle of Lake George: September 8, 1755.* New York: Society of Colonial Wars, 1903.

Flexner, James Thomas. *Lord of the Mohawks: A Biography of Sir William Johnson.* Boston: Little, Brown and Company, 1979.

Folsom, Nathaniel. "Captain Nathaniel Folsom's Fight." In Massachusetts Historical Society, *Proceedings of the Massachusetts Historical Society.* Vol. 18. Boston: published by the society, 1905.

Fowler, William M. *Empires at War: The French and Indian War and the Struggle for North America, 1754–1763.* New York: Walker & Company, 2005.

Gallup, Andrew, ed. *Memoir of a French and Indian War Soldier: "Jolicoeur" Charles Bonin.* Bowie, MD: Heritage Books, Inc., 1993.

Hadden, James. *Washington's Early Campaigns: The French Post Expedition, Great Meadows & Braddock's Defeat.* N.p.: Leonaur Ltd., 2009.

Hall, Dennis Jay, ed. *The Journals of Sir William Johnson's Scouts, 1755 & 1756: The Early Scouts of Robert Rogers & His Rangers Along the Shores of Lake Champlain & Lake George.* Vermont: Essence of Vermont, 1999.

Halpenny, Francess G. *Dictionary of Canadian Biography, 1741–1770.* Vol. 3. Toronto: University of Toronto Press, 1974.

Hamilton, Milton W. *Sir William Johnson: Colonial American, 1715–1763.* Port Washington, NY: Kennikat Press, 1976.

Hill, James. "The Diary of a Private on the First Expedition to Crown Point." Edited by Edna V. Moffett. *The New England Quarterly.* Vol. 5. Boston: New England Quarterly, Inc., 1932.

Hill, William H. *Old Fort Edward, Before 1800: An Account of the Historic Ground Now Occupied by the Village of Fort Edward, New York.* Fort Edward, NY: privately published, 1929.

Hinderaker, Eric. *The Two Hendricks: Unraveling a Mohawk Mystery.* Cambridge, MA: Harvard University Press, 2010.

Historical Society of Pennsylvania. *The Pennsylvania Magazine of History and Biography.* Vol. 3. Philadelphia: self-published, 1879.

Hollister, G.H. *The History of Connecticut, from the First Settlement of the Colony.* Vol. 1. Hartford, CT: L. Stebbins & Company, 1858.

Hook, Richard, and Stuart Reid. *British Redcoat, 1740–1793.* London: Osprey Publishing Ltd., 1996.

Hughes, Ben. *The Siege of Fort William Henry: A Year on the Northeastern Frontier.* Yardley, PA: Westholme Publishing, 2011.

Johnson, Crisfield. *History of Washington County, New York—with Illustrations and Biographical Sketches of Some of Its Prominent Men and Pioneers.* Philadelphia: Everts & Ensign, 1878.

Kemmer, Brenton. *Freeman, Freeholders, and Citizen Soldiers: An Organizational History of Colonel Jonathan Bagley's Regiment, 1755–1760.* Westminster, MD: Heritage Books, Inc., 2011.

————. *Redcoats, Yankees and Allies: A History of the Uniforms, Clothing, and Gear of the British Army in the Lake George–Lake Champlain Corridor, 1755–1760.* Westminster, MD: Heritage Books, Inc., 1998.

Kingsford, William. *The History of Canada, 1726–1756.* Vol. 3. New York: AMS Press, 1968. Reprinted from the edition of 1889.

Lincoln, Charles Henry, ed. *Correspondence of William Shirley, Governor of Massachusetts and Military Commander in America, 1731–1760.* New York: Macmillan Company, 1912.

———. *Manuscript Records of the French and Indian War in the Library of the American Antiquarian Society.* Westminster, MD: Heritage Books Inc., 2007.

Lowell, John. *A Sermon Occasioned for the Most Lamented Death of Col. Moses Titcomb, Who Fell in Battle Near Lake-George, September 8ᵗʰ, 1755.* Boston: Edes and Gill, 1760.

Lucier, Armand Francis. *French and Indian War Notices Abstracted from Colonial Newspapers.* 5 vols. Bowie, MD: Heritage Books, Inc., 2007.

Marston, Daniel. *The French-Indian War, 1754–1760.* Oxford: Osprey Publishing, 2002.

McCardell, Lee. *Ill-Starred General: Braddock of the Coldstream Guards.* Pittsburgh, PA: University of Pittsburgh Press, 1958.

McLoughlin, William G. *Rhode Island: A History.* New York: W.W. Norton & Company, 1986.

Nester, William R. *The Epic Battles for Ticonderoga, 1758.* New York: State University of New York Press, 2008.

New York State Historical Association. *Constitution and By-Laws with Proceedings of the Second Annual Meeting.* New York: New York State Historical Association, 1901.

New York State Historical Society. "Muster Rolls of New York Provincial Troops, 1755–1764." In *Collections of the New-York Historical Society.* Vol. 24. New York: printed for the society, 1892.

O'Callaghan, E.B., ed. *Documents Relative to the Colonial History of the State of New-York.* 10 vols. Albany, NY: Weed, Parsons and Company, 1853–58.

Pargellis, Stanley, ed. *Military Affairs in North America, 1748–1765: Selected Documents from the Cumberland Papers in Windsor Castle.* New York: Archon Books, 1969. Originally published in 1936.

Parkman, Francis. *Montcalm and Wolfe: The French and Indian War.* New York: Barnes & Noble, 2005. Originally published in 1884.

Pew, William A. *Colonel Ephraim Williams: An Appreciation.* Williamstown, MA: Williams College, 1919.

———. *The Drums of Ephraim Williams: A Brief.* Salem, MA: privately printed, 1925.

Peyser, Joseph L, ed. and trans. *Jaques Legardeur de Saint-Pierre: Officer, Gentleman, Entrepreneur.* East Lansing: Michigan State University Press, 1996.

Pomeroy, Seth. *The Journals and Papers of Seth Pomeroy: Sometime General in the Colonial Service*. Edited by Louis Effingham de Forest. New York: Society of Colonial Wars in the State of New York, 1926.

Preston, David. *Braddock's Defeat: The Battle of the Monongahela and the Road to Revolution*. New York: Oxford University Press, 2015.

Reid, Stuart. *The Flintlock Musket: Brown Bess and Charleville, 1715–1865*. Oxford: Osprey Publishing, 2016.

Robert Moses Diary. Gilder Lehrmann Institute of American History, New York. https://www.gilderlehrman.org/collections/cb0a2cd4-e876-4c93-92d2-366324483270.

Roberts, Gary Boyd. *Genealogies of Connecticut Families: From the New England Historical and Genealogy Register*. Vol. 1. Baltimore, MD: Genealogical Publishing Company Inc., 1983.

Ross, John F. *War on the Run: The Epic Story of Robert Rogers and the Conquest of America's First Frontier*. New York: Bantam Books, 2009.

Russell, Carl P. *Guns on the Early Frontiers: From Colonial Times to the Years of the Western Fur Trade*. Mineola, NY: Dover Publications, Inc., 2005. Originally published in 1957.

Schultz, John A. *William Shirley: King's Governor of Massachusetts*. Chapel Hill: University of North Carolina Press, 1961.

Shannon, Timothy J. *Indians and Colonists at the Crossroads of Empire: The Albany Congress of 1754*. Ithaca, NY: Cornell University Press, 2000.

Sheppard, Ruth, ed. *Empires Collide: The French and Indian War, 1754–1763*. New York: Osprey Publishing, 2006.

Society of Colonial Wars in the Commonwealth of Massachusetts. *Society of Colonial Wars in the Commonwealth of Massachusetts*. No. 8. Boston: printed for the society, 1906.

Starbuck, David R. *The Great Warpath: British Military Sites from Albany to Crown Point*. Hanover, NH: University Press of New England, 1999.

————. *Massacre at Fort William Henry*. Hanover, NH: University Press of New England, 2002.

Stark, James Henry. *The Loyalists of Massachusetts and the Other Side of the American Revolution*. Salem, MA: Salem Press Company, 1910.

Steele, Ian K. *Betrayals: Fort William Henry & the "Massacre."* New York: Oxford University Press, 1990.

Stevens, Phillip H. *Artillery through the Ages*. New York: Franklin Watts, Inc., 1965.

Sullivan, James, ed. *The Papers of Sir William Johnson*. 14 vols. Albany: University of the State of New York, 1922.

Todish, Timothy J. *The Annotated and Illustrated Journals of Major Robert Rogers.* Fleischmanns, NY: Purple Mountain Press, 2002.

Trumball, James Russell, *History of Northampton, Massachusetts: From its Settlement in 1654.* Vol. 2. Northampton, MA: Press of Gazette Printing Company, 1902.

Tucker, Spencer C., ed. *The Encyclopedia of North American Colonial Conflicts to 1775: A Political, Social, and Military History.* 3 vols. Santa Barbara, CA: ABC-CLIO, 2008.

Van Rensselaer, Cortlandt. *An Historical Discourse on the Occasion of the Centennial Celebration of the Battle of Lake George, 1755.* Philadelphia: published by request, 1856.

Wade, Mason, ed. *The Journals of Francis Parkman.* 2 vols. New York: Harper & Brothers Publishers, 1947.

Whiting, Nathaniel. "Letters of Colonel Nathan Whiting." In *Papers of the New Haven Colony Historical Society.* Vol. 6. New Haven, CT: New Haven Colony Historical Society, 1900.

Williams, Noel St. John. *Redcoats Along the Hudson: The Struggle for North America, 1754–1763.* London: Brassey's, 1998.

INDEX

Stark, John 35
St. Clair, John 51
St. Frédéric (Crown Point) 12
St. Pierre, Jacques Legardeur 74,
    92

Wolfe, James 103
Wraxall, Peter 87, 91, 93, 96

T

Titcomb, Moses 30, 31, 66, 94, 101
Treaty of Aix-la-Chappelle 54
Treaty of Paris 103
Treaty of Utrecht 54

V

Vaudreuil de Cavagnal, Pierre
    Francois 42
Vergor, Louis Du Pont Duchambon
    56
Virginia
  Alexandria 15, 16, 19
  Williamsburg 15
  Winchester 50

W

Warren, Peter 25
Washington, George 22, 48, 52
West Virginia
  Shepherdstown 51
Whiting, Nathan 66, 87, 101
William Johnson 30
  Carlyle House Congress 19
Williams College 103
Williams, Ephraim 22, 30, 31, 86,
    101, 103
Williams, Thomas 94, 107
Winslow, John 54

ABOUT THE AUTHOR

William R. Griffith IV is a native of Branchburg, New Jersey, and a 2014 graduate of Shepherd University in Shepherdstown, West Virginia, with a degree in history. While conducting his undergraduate studies he concentrated in the Civil War and nineteenth-century America but independently focused on all aspects of American military history. His passion for the French and Indian War was born when he visited his first historic site, Fort William Henry, at the age of five. After annual family vacations to Lake George, he continued to harbor a strong passion for the region's colonial history. Griffith is the cofounder of *The Great Task Remaining* history blog (www.gtrhistory.com), which desires to give future historians a voice in the online community by displaying their work for the general public. Along with writing for his own blog, he has been published in *Garden State Legacy* magazine, the *U.S. Navy Cruiser Sailors Association* and periodical *Emerging Civil War*'s online blog and has conducted numerous lectures and presentations for various history and genealogy groups throughout New Jersey. He has previously worked for the David Library of the American Revolution and Fort Frederick State Park in Big Pool, Maryland, as a historical interpreter. He led tours at the George Spangler Farm Field Hospital Site in Gettysburg, Pennsylvania, during the battle's 150th anniversary summer. When he is not studying history, William spends his time devotedly following his second passion, the New York Yankees.